Nancy
Hale

on the life & work

of a lost american master

Nancy
Hale

on the life & work

of a lost american master

Dan Chaon, Norah Hardin Lind, & Phong Nguyen, Editors

The Unsung Masters Series at Pleiades Press
Warrensburg, Missouri, 2012

Contents

Introduction

Dan Chaon

—∞∞∞—

I am the proud owner of four collections of stories by Nancy Hale. All of them are out of print and difficult to find—you have to scour the websites of used booksellers—and the edition I have of one of her greatest books, *The Earliest Dreams*, is a hoary specimen from 1936 that I feel nervous about when I turn its 75-year-old pages because they are a bit brittle and I am afraid the spine will break apart.

This is crazy, in my opinion. Nancy Hale was one of the most accomplished and decorated American short story writers of her time. Her stories appeared four times in *The Best American Short Stories* anthology, ten times in the *O. Henry* anthology, and she holds the record for an author who has published the most stories in *The New Yorker* in a single year (12 stories, between July of 1954 and July of 1955). Yet it appears that most readers of short stories—even avid readers—have never even heard her name.

I first encountered Hale's stories in my mid-twenties. I had decided that I was going to read the entire collection of *The Best American Short Stories* series, from 1915 to the present, and thus teach myself something about the history of the form in the twentieth century. I had plowed through a lot of stories by the time I reached the 1935 volume, most of them rather fusty and forgettable.

But I remember my first experience with Hale. It was a story called "The Double House," a tale of a deeply depressed, bullied schoolboy that surprised me with its emotional intensity and acuity.

> "Aunt Esther wanted to be good to her nephew, but Robert tried not to be alone with her since the time, about a year ago, when he was ten, when she had looked at him with tears in her eyes, and shaken her head, and said that he was lucky to be a child, for childhood was the only happy time. At that Robert's heart had stood still with fear, for if it were true that he would never be any happier than he was now, then he was lost."

The story proceeds to follow young Robert through his days, enfolding us in a dreamlike world of childhood loneliness and dread that builds to a feverish pitch. I read it feeling as if I'd discovered some kind of secret cache. *Wait*, I thought. *Who is this writer?*

Which brought me to Hale's first book of stories, *The Earliest Dreams*, a quiet, mysterious, wonder of a book that seems to me a forgotten masterpiece. The stories share a dense, dark, almost phantasmagorical mood—somewhere in the territory between Katherine Mansfield and Ray Bradbury. In "To the Invader," a young pregnant woman finds herself growing increasingly unhinged living in the aristocratic Southern mansion of her mother-in-law; "Midsummer" tells the story of a teenaged girl's first crush with a tone of ominous hysteria that makes her emotional state seem akin to demonic possession; and then there is the title story, "The Earliest Dreams."

Rereading that story still wrecks me. Written in the lilting, hypnotic rhythm of a fairy tale, it is one of the most vivid and honest portraits of childhood I've ever encountered. It evokes a universal experience, that of a child listening to the sound of an adult party from a distance, from a silent bedroom, though it is also utterly specific and grounded. Using an odd and intimate second-person voice, it slowly unravels a single, obsessive memory, and through that memory uncovers a deep sense of the fathomless passage of time. It ends not with an epiphany but with the opposite of an epiphany—an uncanny glimpse into an unknowable mystery, hidden in a quotidian moment. "You never knew what things they laughed at when they laughed so long in the evenings, and now you will never know." Now you will never know: a realization that, to a child, would seem incomprehensible, but to the adult looking back strikes a note of profound loss. *Never.*

If you ever have the opportunity to read *The Earliest Dreams* from beginning to end, I feel certain that you will be as mesmerized as I have been.

~

Hale's subsequent three collections are similarly accomplished, and continue her exploration of memory, childhood, extreme emotional states and mental illness, motherhood, and the lives of women. Stories from *Between the Dark and the Daylight* (1943) also address the mood of the homefront during WWII: In "The Japanese Garden," a mother watches with growing sorrow as her young son becomes obsessed with war and killing and hatred; in "Those Are as Brothers," a tender friendship grows between an abused wife and a Jewish refugee who works as a gardener.

One of my favorite of Hale's stories from this collection, "Who Lived and Died Believing," is one of Hale's longest and strangest. Using a divided perspective, the story moves back and forth between a mental patient who is being prepared to receive shock treatments, and her young nurse, who is struggling with her romance with a medical student. Though it wouldn't be entirely correct to call it a horror story, it is a nightmarish piece—in the contrast between the deranged and desperate female patient and her gently distracted nurse; in the portrayal of the casual application of electroshock therapy; in its chilling final vision, which leaves the unnamed patient

> "crying quietly, for all that was dead, now, forever, and could never be brought back. And it was fading fast. Fade far away, dissolve, and quite forget what thou, among the leaves, hast never known… Above their heads where they sat upon the grass the little leaves whispered. It was all gone, and from now on the world was new, a page unwritten."

~

The Empress's Ring (1953) is particularly remarkable for Hale's exploration of the fictional sketch—very short pieces which, in some ways, seem to look forward to the miniaturism of writers like Amy Hempel. The title story is a great example of this mode: using a simple childhood incident as a way of reflecting on the passage of time and the inevitability of loss, Hale compresses an entire lifetime into five pages. She uses a similar method in the marvelous "The Readville Stars," a story which discards plot in favor of three thematically linked moments in the life of a woman, each one revealing a moment in which a vain, romantic wish is revealed in its hollowness.

Despite the brevity of these pieces, *The Empress's Ring* is one of Hale's most stylistically and thematically varied books. "The Bubble" for example, takes a brassy, ironical, seemingly comic first-person narrator, and pushes it toward darkness and loneliness; "But One Buttonhole Needful" focuses on a single "moment of being" as a mother reads her sick son stories, opening a seemingly innocuous moment into a glimpse of unacknowledged despair; "The Place and the Time" makes use of a startling and hallucinatory flashback instead of a traditional climax.

The Empress's Ring also shows Hale beginning to experiment with the lines between fiction and non-fiction. She includes the following note at the beginning of the book:

> The pieces in this collection called "The Copley-Plaza" and "The First Day of School," although some of their details are fictional, are founded upon fact and are autobiographical; all the other stories (including those written in the first person), although some of their details may be factual, are works of fiction.

These fine distinctions are intriguing, albeit a little puzzling. But they would lead Hale toward a greater exploration of the issues of memory, truth, and autobiography, which would become central concerns in her short-story/memoir collections *A New England Girlhood* (1958) and *The Life in the Studio* (1969), both of which would grapple with the reliability of remembered detail, and the question of what separated memory and fiction.

~

The Pattern of Perfection (1960) was to be Hale's final book of stories, though she continued to write and publish short fiction well into the 1970s. Of her four collections, it is her most traditional; the stories have a genteel, reserved gloss that was typical of *New Yorker* stories of the period. They tend to be longer and more conservative than her previous work, though they remain passionately interested in the workings of memory, time and self-delusion.

"A Slow Boat to China," one of the strongest pieces in the book, is a good example of this new approach. The story of a mother driving her son back to boarding school for the last year before he graduates, the piece is a study of calm surfaces and unspoken tensions as the awkwardness between the pair becomes increasingly strained. "Entrance into Life," included in this volume, is another story of mothers and sons—a brief and piercing sketch in which a woman becomes aware that her chronically ill boy may never live to grow up.

The collection ends with the haunting "Rich People," a piece that reminds me of Alice Munro at the height of her powers. It follows young Lucy Eliot during the summer before college. Lucy becomes enchanted by a wealthy, cosmopolitan neighbor, Mrs. Bogden, who sets out to remake Lucy as an ingénue. The resulting exploration of class, manners, and manipulation is a kind of Henry James novel in miniature; and then, as in many of Hale's greatest stories, the piece takes another turn, and makes a great leap forward in time, and suddenly, as at the end of "The Earliest Dreams," the story looks back on itself from a different perspective. Now, Lucy herself is close to middle-aged, and by chance she encounters the now-ancient Mrs. Bogden on a cruise ship.

> "But the look in the still-beautiful, pleasure-loving, powdered old face stopped me while I peered, hesitating. The look was a double look, really; it was two things at once. Part of it was fear, under the cream foundation…and part of it was death, holding a whip and looking at me, right there out of her face."

Later, as Lucy tries to sleep, she can't stop imagining Mrs. Bogden:

> "My mind went back to Clam Harbor and the days when I was young. Once more, I seemed to be sitting on the silvery splintered boards of the old dock in the morning cool, talking to Mrs. Bogden…. Her face is turned away toward the sea,

but... I could hear her voice asking me, as I have so often heard her ask, 'The way to be happy is always to be in love, isn't it? Isn't it?' She turns her lovely face toward me, and this time her face is full of death."

~

It is a great privilege to be able to re-introduce Nancy Hale to a new generation of readers, thanks to the Pleiades Press Unsung Masters series. It's especially exciting to see seven of her wonderful stories back in print for the first time in many years; and I hope that it might spur enough interest that we might soon see a full book of "selected stories," since there were far too many wonderful pieces to include all in this volume.

More than anything, I hope that this sample might inspire readers to seek out Hale's beautiful collections of stories— which are not simply "collections," but books in their own right: living, breathing creations that immerse the reader in a strange and wonderfully mysterious vision of the world.

As a writer and a reader, I have learned a great deal from Nancy Hale. She put her spell upon me. If you let her, she will do the same for you.

2012

The Influence of Art on Nancy Hale

Norah Hardin Lind

———∽∾∾———

During the early decades of *The New Yorker* magazine, the short stories of Nancy Hale appeared with a regularity that acted as a shaping force, defining the young publication. Her narratives provided a cultural account of the changing role of women in 1930s New York, and her novels tackled new subjects by depicting the complex lives of a series of brazen young women. She shared the attention and encouragement of legendary Scribner's editor Maxwell Perkins with Ernest Hemingway, F. Scott Fitzgerald, and Thomas Wolfe. Despite tremendous recognition during her lifetime, including ten O. Henry awards, Nancy Hale's star had faded by the time of her death in 1988. Her longtime friend, *The New Yorker* editor William Maxwell, wrote at Hale's death that "it must have seemed to her that her work, in later years, had gone largely unappreciated. At the moment Willa Cather isn't read as much as she once was. One can depend on time to correct myopia of this kind." [1]

---

[1] "Tribute" 227

Reflecting on Nancy Hale's writing necessarily evokes her life, for despite any claims she made to the contrary, her work is largely autobiographical. She writes of her remarkable artistic family, successful career years, troubled marriages, and emotional breakdowns. The author is present in the characters who fill her narratives—often youthful and lovely women from privileged social backgrounds. Hale's precise descriptions shape with warmth the world that she knew. She builds characters, settings, and scenes through astonishing sensory detail, allowing the audience to share her world—a skill that was nurtured during a childhood of engagement with literature and art, and by a family which for generations counted among its members some of the most significant creative professionals in America. The thought processes of the visual artist creep through Hale's writing, bringing vital images to readers who followed her work.

Despite Nancy Hale's early recognition as a writer during her academic career at Boston's Winsor School, she followed graduation with two years of study at the School of the Museum of Fine Arts, Boston. Her father, Philip Hale, was a prominent instructor there throughout her childhood. Her mother, Lilian Westcott Hale, gained recognition within the respected Boston School of artists during its heyday.

In reviewing Nancy Hale's memoir of life with her parents entitled *The Life in the Studio*, Diana Loercher notes: "Artists have grown like leaves on the family tree." [2] Certainly, Nancy Hale's life was surrounded by art. Her mother moved her studio into their home when Nancy was born, maintaining the decorum of a maternal image while pursuing her art. Philip Hale sketched during the evenings after his days of instructing art, or he worked on one of the many articles, books or lectures about art that he produced to supplement his wages from the museum school.

---

[2] Loercher 22

Despite the proliferation of Hale artists working around the turn of the century, the popular historian Van Wyck Brooks describes a more widely recognized family attribute in *The Flowering of New England 1815-1865*: "To write a book for one of the Hales, was as natural as to breathe ... [They] were all authors by instinct." [3] Philip Hale's father Edward Everett Hale, well-known patriarch of the Boston Brahmin family, was arguably the most powerful figure in Boston at the turn of the century. Edward Everett Hale led a large congregation before his appointment as the chaplain of the senate. Of his prolific writings, perhaps the most recognized titles are *A New England Boyhood* and "The Man without a Country."

The abilities of the family's women were respected as well, and provided proof positive for Nancy Hale that women were capable of writing; indeed, in the Hale family, they were expected to write. Her grandfather Edward Everett Hale enlisted the skills of family members, including daughter Ellen Day Hale, to meet his formidable literary obligations. His sister, Lucretia Peabody Hale, published numerous works in her own name, including *The Peterkin Papers*. Edward Everett Hale's wife was the niece of Harriet Beecher Stowe, author of *Uncle Tom's Cabin*—the best-selling and arguably the most politically influential book of the 19th century. Her own niece was the struggling feminist writer Charlotte Perkins Gilman.

Nancy Hale absorbed the paired influences of visual art and literature, and the marriage of the two forms provides the descriptive quality that distinguishes her writing. Because of the Hale family's significance to the early history of New England, their correspondence is archived in a number of libraries. Within these records, the combination of visual art and text is apparent in the correspondence of various Hale family members who enhance their letters with sketches of daily life. Nancy

[3] *The Flowering of New England* 499

Hale said that "people who can do one art can usually do one or more of the others," but few of Hale's contemporaries possessed her deep level of understanding of the visual arts. [4]

Her father's career clearly embraced the family's convergence of skills. Philip Hale was a painter and a writer, and his critical reviews and books on visual art led him eventually to supplement his instructor duties with popular public lectures on art topics. All of these pursuits were assumed to fulfill the obligation that he felt to support his small family. He recognized his wife as the superior artist, and rather than challenging her success, he insisted that the family employ a household helper so that Lilian Westcott Hale might devote herself to her artwork. The thorough shaping influence of art and artists led Nancy Hale to title her book of reflections about her parents *The Life in the Studio*. In that collection of stories, which focused on her life as the only child of two artists, she relies upon the critical eye that she developed living with them, to record visual effects in highly sensory terms—with the nuance of an artist.

Hale captures a moment, an image, a character, or a scene through visual descriptions that reflect a childhood surrounded by art. In a story from *The Life in the Studio*, she describes a distinguishing feature of her role in the household—her repeated service as a model:

> My mother had drawn me at the age of six weeks in my bassinet; propped up against pillows, at the age of six months, on a background of patterned roses. At the age of one, seated in a baby carriage [...] I had to pose so much in my childhood that when I reached the age of about thirteen I finally figured out a requirement of my own. I wouldn't pose, I said, unless I could be painted with a book. So all subsequent pictures show me in the act of reading [...] some show the book, some don't; but all have the eyes downcast.[5]

---

[4] Loercher 22

[5] *The Life in the Studio* 18-19

This control of her situation provided her with hours of reading time. The writing habit followed naturally, according to family tradition. As a young child, she surprised her mother by asking for a printing press for Christmas, and Philip assured his wife that most Hale children requested printing presses during childhood. By the age of eight, Nancy was producing a family newspaper. She published her first story in the *Boston Herald* at age eleven for the purpose, she said, of remuneration. Surrounded by the tools of both trades, the young Nancy Hale may have felt that only two professions were open to her. She chose to write, but her parents' devotion to art profoundly influenced her writing. In a tribute to Nancy Hale after her death in 1988, William Maxwell reflected on her use of the senses in her descriptions. He noted the continual influence Hale's childhood exposure to art played on her writing. Maxwell references the popular story "Midsummer," recognized by the staff at *The New Yorker* as one of the finest stories the magazine had yet published:

> The child of painters, Nancy Hale was brought up in a world where it was inconceivable that beauty of one kind or another would not be an essential part of her art. Her writing reflects this assumption. Her descriptive powers are remarkable but seldom used in the service of the merely visual. For example: "The sound of the horses' feet was like a confused heartbeat on the swampy ground. They both felt it. They used to get off their horses, without having said a word, and helplessly submerge themselves in each other's arms, while the sweat ran down their backs under their shirts." Writing like that doesn't age.[6]

Her early novels were handled by the legendary Scribner's editor Maxwell Perkins, who was so certain of Hale's ability that he published her two early novels to retain her on the company's literary clients' list for the day when he sensed her true gift would emerge. Both of Hale's first two novels made little impact, but

---

[6] "Tribute" 226-7

Perkins related to mutual friend Elizabeth Lemmon that he instantly recognized in Hale a writer of unusual talent: "—like you Virginians think a colt could run when he could barely stand. So I watched her and got us to publish her when she couldn't sell. Now she has a great name in the magazines, but she hasn't yet sold for us. So I want to be vindicated." [7]

Nancy Hale was fortunate to find an editor as understanding as Maxwell Perkins. She maintained a routine whenever possible, and her stories flowed in a steady stream to publication. She clearly outshone both of her first two husbands, who were also writers, and the resulting personal conflicts contributed to the only significant interruptions in her writing—the troubling emotional breakdowns which rendered her physically and mentally drained. With the patience and understanding of a psychologist, Perkins supported Hale through each crisis, receiving his vindication with her 1942 best seller, *The Prodigal Women*, which Hale referred to as the story of her second marriage.

Hale struggled to come to terms with her failed relationships in *The Prodigal Women*, but she also experienced difficulty coping with the novel's large scale. She wrote to William Maxwell, whom she referred to as "a kind of artistic conscience"[8]:

> "The whole scale is so big and you have to keep your mind on the big side, the whole picture, and somehow you can't also write in careful detail; I mean you can't write the kind of accurate semll-and-sound [sic] stuff that I know I can sometimes do well, but must write on a larger, looser scale of which I am unsure . . ." [9]

Her editor, Maxwell Perkins, sympathized with her difficulties in writing *The Prodigal Women*, but for different reasons than the length. He wrote to her on Oct. 21, 1942:

---

[7] Berg 206

[8] NHP, SSC, 14.20, 1943

[9] NHP, SSC, 14.20, undated letter

I know that this book was a very hard book, for specific reasons, and that it was one of those books that a writer must get out and get through with before she can go on. But I am getting more satisfaction, and just as much pleasure from your triumph, even upon egoistic grounds alone—for, from the very beginning, I believed in you and said so, and while I don't believe that sales are in themselves a proof, they are the only proof and the irrefutable proof to a lot of people to whom I have to say things—booksellers and such. So don't thank me for any pleasure. It is I who must thank you.[10]

The publication of *The Prodigal Women* was followed by the longest interruption to Hale's writing career, resulting from an emotional breakdown. She found the short story form more comfortable, allowing her to exercise the stylistic precision which brought her a sense of control. The incorporation of her artistic eye in producing short narratives lent a painterly nuance to the visions that she brought to the audience, layering her language like brush-strokes on a canvas. Hale's stories encourage mental imaging, providing details which color and texture the thoughts. She speaks to the reader's eyes. Artistic hybridity dominates *The Life in the Studio*. The collection of linked stories opens with a visual description of the studio that Hale felt compelled to clean out following her mother's death, which demonstrates her painterly technique:

> All this accumulation is of no immediate use to anyone alive today. "All this junk," my husband calls it, as he views the half-empty pots of glue and linseed oil and turpentine; the balsa-wood plane models, broken, my son made while my mother was painting him; coils of wire used on boats for some purpose; cigar boxes of dried-up paint tubes; the conch shells in the still-life composition that was the last thing my mother painted before she died; the rotted leather

[10] Perkins 206-7

trunks full of photographs mounted on cards in the Victorian manner, of ladies in bustles, gentlemen with beards, once somebody's friends but now forever unknown; a yellow luster vase; a pair of desiccated rubber gloves for handling the etching plates in an acid bath; a pile of old *Transactions of the Bronte Society*; several palettes, still set, the blobs of paint dried as hard as multicolored marbles; plaster casts, damaged, of Aphrodite, of a della Robbia bambino, or an écorché—a model of the nude stripped to show the muscles; a pile of oil pochades my father painted on one of his infrequent visits away from his Boston studio . . . [11]

Roberta White writes of such work, that "descriptive passages are analogs of painting, composed visual impressions that do more than provide a setting; they arrest moments in time and offer a perceptual point of view…." [12] Nancy Hale, the writer and the artist, provides a clear visual image through words. Her list captures the look of the studio as surely as her parents conceived compositions with their brushes. Here we encounter her textural description: "rotted leather trunks," "desiccated rubber gloves," and "blobs of paint dried as hard as multi-colored marbles." The value in these objects of dry decay has ended like her parents' lives, also marking the loss of Nancy Hale's childhood world. Her words preserve the studio forever; she is a sensitive participant, recreating the visual world as text, poignantly reflecting on the past through images like the pictures of Victorian men and women—"once somebody's friends but now forever unknown…." [12]

Years after Hale wrote about her parents, Doubleday commissioned her to write about another artist's life; however, her view of Mary Cassatt could not be shaped by intimate experiences like those that Hale had shared with her parents. She had

---

[11] *The Life in the Studio* 3-4

[12] White 76

never met Cassatt; how was she to understand how this artist worked and thought? Hale writes in the book's prologue that she was forced to seek the artist by studying her paintings, looking for what the pictures revealed about the artist: "It was not that her pictures told about her, so much that they *were* her; just as the other side of the moon, hidden, is still the moon." [13] Hale's analysis of Cassatt's paintings, however, falls short of a truly penetrating insight into the artist. She did attempt to enter the world of Mary Cassatt in her own honest way—through direct experience. Traveling to Paris to research the Cassatt book, Hale visited the painter's favorite places. She sat on the sidewalk outside Cassatt's favorite café, in all likelihood sipping the artist's favorite tipple while watching passersby. She traveled in Cassatt's footsteps before facing the task of presenting the artist to her readers. Hale wrote of the effort:

> [W]e talked to a variety of locals—peasants in wooden sabots standing deep in barnyard muck, old women wrapped in the ubiquitous shawl of France as they leaned against a cold wind sweeping down the village street. An hour was spent with the granddaughter of Reine, the cook-model Mary Cassatt painted so often. Again and again I was struck, less by the fact that so few of them had in fact met the artist, than by the way their faces would fall as they themselves became aware that, no, they never actually spoke with l'Imperatrice; but Yes!—the faces would brighten—they had seen her often, out in front of the chateau among the rose bushes. All were of one mind that they had, without doubt, known Mary Cassatt, known her well. For all the unsentimentality of the French, it was plain that Mary Cassatt was a living presence, like the images in religion, a sort of local saint. In speaking of her they seldom used her name; she was the Benefactor, the Lady of the chateau, the American. She was *l'Imperatrice*.[14]

---

[13] *Mary Cassatt: A Biography of the Great American Painter* xxv
[14] Ibid. 289

Again Hale paints her own picture for the audience, first of the peasants, then, relying on their accounts, she provides a sketchy image of the artist—not with paint, but with her own textual medium. Theorist W.J.T. Mitchell describes the type of interplay that Hale maintains between the visual and the textual: "Images always appear in some material medium—paint, film, stone, electronic impulses, or paper. And yet a crucial feature of the lives of images is their ability to circulate from one medium to another, to move from the page to the screen, from the screen to the performances of everyday life, and back to the page." [15] Hale connects the artist's and the writer's forms through visual narratives.

The ability to capture the visual in text is the hallmark of Nancy Hale's technical skill and her stylistic strength, yet she felt that her parents experienced the visual in a manner superior to her own. She describes her mother's visual sensitivity:

> When my mother looked at things (and her life was given over to looking at things; in any unfamiliar house she used to keep crying "Look at that! Look at that! About a chair, a picture, a china bowl of flowers, until she became embarrassed by the realization that nobody else joined her), she looked with a kind of innocent, once-born stare. I can see that now, too. She held her eyes very wide open and simply stared, as though confronted by the first day of creation. Often she saw things quite differently from other people. Colors, for instance, appeared different to her from what they seemed to me to be. She would keep talking about a blue house on the road to Gloucester, and I couldn't imagine what she was talking about, and then one day we would be driving that road together and she would cry, "There's the blue house! Look at that." I would look, and it would be white.
>
> "You're so *literary*," my father and mother used to complain to me. This was in no sense a compliment but

[15] Mitchell 294

referred to the instantaneous reflex of reading into color what I figured it had to be, instead of seeing it for what—in that light—it was.[16]

If Hale was less visually sensitive than her artist parents, she compensated through a heightened awareness of her other senses. In "My Mother's Solitudes," for example, she describes a day spent home from school sick. She constructs her recollections the way an artist plans the details of a composition. Rather than relying on visual elements, Hale highlights her separation from her mother at work in the studio, through careful attention to sound rather than sight. That is the only part of her mother accessible to her in her illness:

> From far away in the back of the house came faint domestic sounds—the coal range being shaken down, the black iron door to the oven opened and shut. I have no recollections of the hum of a vacuum cleaner. Somehow things got done about the house, but not by my mother. Her mornings were, properly, for work. The sounds of her working made a principal part of that tiny accenting to the snowy silence, and I could identify each sound.
>
> There was the sharp, steady sawing of charcoal (sharpened to a needle point with a razor blade) up and down against the sheet of Strathmore board on my mother's easel as she worked on a snow scene from the windows of the front hall that, with the aid of a wardrobe and a chest of drawers, my father used as a dressing room. There would come a pause in the sawing, and a faint rattle, while she rummaged around in the blue-edged box that French charcoal came in. A clack—she had dropped something on the floor. If it was charcoal, it fell with a small explosion. Then a scratchy, rubbing sound, which was the careful filing of the sides of her stick of charcoal against the board covered with fine sandpaper which had a handle to keep one's fingers clean. A pause. Then would recommence the sawing

---

[16] *The Life in the Studio* 21-22

of the point drawn rhythmically up and down. I would go back to Miss Brontë, or make a stab at arithmetic, but every now and then I would give myself over again to rest in the long morning's stillness.

Sometime near noon, the day's letters would come pouring in through the slot in the front door, onto the hall floor, with a splash.[17]

This particular passage relies heavily on the sense of sound as Nancy Hale creates a picture by writing through senses unavailable to the artist. She records the quiet in another description of an afternoon with her mother:

We sat together then for a while before she got up to make tea, in one of those long silences when tiny sounds become brilliantly distinct—the occasional *clunk* of the electric clock on the wall of the kitchenette in that small, peaceful apartment; the creak, as my great-grandfather's sea chest in the parlor settled a bit; the sound of a chunk of wet snow as it slid off the roof onto more wet snow; the sound of a car passing outside, coming to us muffled, as though from far away.[18]

The technical element that defines Hale's writing is the blend of senses in her descriptions. She conveys scenes with the details of an astute observer. Here she relies on smell to describe the delights of the studio:

[W]hen I would come in from a swim or a walk on the moors, on entering the studio I could smell distinctly not only the oil paint and turpentine from my mother's reign but, rising from the layers of years upon years, the nitric acid used in solution to bite the etching plates of my old aunt who had built the studio back in 1911.

Once or twice, to my astonishment, I burst into tears. What astonished me was not so much that I should be crying as what, I realized, I was crying about. It was not because

[17] *The Life in the Studio* 39
[18] Ibid. 43-44

my mother or Aunt Nelly was dead, or out of sadness for all those other artists, Aunt Nelly's friends, who also used the place long ago; but because, in the silence of the studio, I remembered what a wonderful time they all had.[19]

Raymond Carver, who died the same year as Hale, wrote that a writer should avoid gimmicks in writing, favoring instead the act of viewing the world and handing that world over to the reader in his own unique way. The Hale method was a nuanced blend of sensory images rendered with the technical precision of a master craftsman—of an artist. This particular aspect of Nancy Hale's writing is perhaps the reason that her short stories outshine her novels. She captures glimpses of life—frequently her own life. Hale commented in a speech that while her autobiographical writing is rooted in reality, it is created with awareness that the perceptions will be shared. The author's purpose is to bring the reader to a sense of identification with the writing, to make the reader a part of it.[20] The life of the author contributes to the process, but the reaction of the audience, Hale felt, was the measure of a work's success. Hale cautioned others about the importance of the reader's position in the process:

> [Y]our life is important, it is serious and tragic and pathetic and frustrated, right down the line. But if you are going to make it seem in the slightest degree important to that sea of blank faces, your possible public, it has got to be on their terms. They are viewing you coldly from outside. [21]

Whether writing with humor or poignancy, Hale shares a depth of perception with her readers that results from her own instinctive recording of observations. She persists in her

---

[19] Ibid. 99-100

[20] NHP, SSC, 26.2, card 26

[21] NHP, SSC, 26.2, card 16

effort at clear recall even when the struggle is hindered by the pain of childbirth and the era's efforts to eliminate that discomfort with drugs. Lilian Westcott Hale wrote to her sister-in-law, Ellen Day Hale, about Nancy's first labor in March of 1930: "He came on the exact day he was expected at one minute past one daytime and while it was a rather long process, Nancy said she didn't mind it a bit." The letter continues that despite morphine and gas,

> She was very keen about trying to remember what it was all like and all the sensations. She described them to me the day after and she is going to write them down when she is allowed to sit up. She has asked so many people what the thing was like and they always answer that they can't remember! [22]

Nancy Hale records the sensations in "The Bubble," a heavily autobiographical account of childbirth:

> I said, "I know what this pain feels like. It feels as if I were in a dark tunnel that was too small for me, and I were trying to squeeze through it to get to the end, where I can see a little light."
> The doctor laughed, "That's not what you're doin'," he said. "That's what the baby's doin.'"
> But that was the way it felt, all the same [....]
> But I was feeling very strong and full of power. I was working my way down that long tunnel that was too tight for me, down toward the little light that showed at the far end. Then I had a terrible pain. That's all I'm going to stand, I thought calmly. Deliberately I opened my mouth and screamed. [23]

Nancy Hale's short stories are snatches of life largely drawn from her own experience, which open possibilities for

---

[22] NHP, SSC, 98.15

[23] *The Empress's Ring* 35-36

the audience. Hale attempts to evoke memories and thereby provide the members of the audience with a sense of belonging in the world. In Hale's words, "offering a seat to them in that same boat we are all in."[24] In *A New England Girlhood*, which she wrote in response to her grandfather Edward Everett Hale's *A New England Boyhood*, Nancy Hale comments in her introduction on a reader's response to her story about losing a ring in childhood. She recalls:

> I did not, moreover, own a ring that once belonged to the Empress of Austria; the ring I did own [...] I never lost. Things did get lost; and that I was not the only child to lose and mourn something indefinably precious was demonstrated to me by such letters as the one from a man in Canada, who said "I too lost something, when I was six—the little pearl-handled knife my father had given me. I know how you felt about losing your ring, and I know you are only calling it a ring."[25]

Hale recreates and shares universal human emotions. Her rich description brings incidents to life, but it is her expression of feeling that provokes the audience's response. She wrote in a speech:

> [P]eople do like to get together and have a good talk about their youths. Nobody listens to anybody else, except to be reminded of something that happened to them when they were ten. I have come to believe that this is a basic impulse. For the writer of autobiography it means something important: that here is something in readers which can be reached, an instinct to share memories, a desire to compare notes on living.[26]

Hale revives for her readers moments which are universal in nature, allowing them to reflect on a past incident in a fresh light.

---

[24] NHP, SSC, 26.2, card 29

[25] *A New England Girlhood* xvi

[26] NHP, SSC, 26.2, card 28

She writes of the glimmers of old memory that fill her stories of childhood, "What interested me in writing them was to try to catch the reverberations from childhood that sometimes make it seem as if the first few years of all our lives constitute a riddle which it is a lifework to solve." [27] Nancy Hale was guided by her desire to translate her sharp visual acuity onto the printed page. The effort brought her deep into her own past, reviewing times of sadness and joy and regret. In a tribute at Hale's death, John Frederick Nims quoted from a letter that she had written to him: " 'Isn't it extraordinary how easy it is to not remember the past but just plain be in the past, for an hour or a half an hour? I mean it's all in the mind, but so is now.'" [28] Nancy Hale's ability to look back and capture the freshness of a moment is the hallmark of her fiction.

William Maxwell, by reputation a tough editor, considered Hale's writing "flawless" in technique and revealing in its subject matter, which he called "the bedrock of human experience." [29] Hale provided the readers of her era a clear vision of her world—a world so easily related to their own. Her glimmers of recollection provide the reader a sense of belonging in the world. Hale describes the sense of community she inspires, as like ". . . sitting on some cosmic front porch together, rocking, exchanging long, gratifying accounts of our happy or unhappy lives. At any moment the writer is trying to make it seem that the reader can break in upon the writer's stream of discourse crying, 'Why that is just the way it was with me!'" [30] It is difficult in writing about Hale, to limit the selection of excerpts from her work. Each seems to say more, to show more than the last, revealing universal images, glimpses from each of our lives.

---

[27] *A New England Girlhood* xvi

[28] "Tribute" 227

[29] Ibid.

[30] NHP, SSC, 26.2, card 31

Works Cited

Berg, A. Scott. *Max Perkins: Editor of Genius.* London: Hamish Hamilton, 1979.

Brooks, Van Wyck. *The Flowering of New England 1815-1865.* New York: Dutton, 1952.

Hale, Nancy. *The Empress's Ring.* New York: Scribner's, 1955.

—————. *The Life in the Studio.* Boston: Little, Brown, 1969.

—————. *Mary Cassatt: A Biography of the Great American Painter* Garden City, NY: Doubleday, 1975. xxii-xxvii.

—————. Introduction. *A New England Girlhood.* Boston: Little, Brown, 1958.

Loercher, Diana. "Nancy Hale: disciplined biographer." *The Christian Science Monitor.* 3 Sept. 1975. 22.

Maxwell, William. "A Tribute." In "Nancy Hale." Anne Hobson Freeman. *Dictionary of Literary Biography Yearbook: 1988.* Ed. J. M. Brook. Detroit: Gale, 1989. 226-227.

Mitchell, W.J.T.. *What Do Pictures Want? The Lives and Loves of Images.* Chicago: U of Chicago P, 2005.

Nancy Hale Papers. Sophia Smith Collection, Smith College, Northampton, MA.

Nims, John Frederick. "A Tribute." In "Nancy Hale." Anne Hobson Freeman. *Dictionary of Literary Biography Yearbook 1988.* Ed. J. M. Brook. Detroit: Gale, 1989. 227-228.

Perkins, Maxwell E. *Editor to Author: The Letters of Maxwell E. Perkins.* Ed. John Hall Wheelock. New York and London: Scribner's, 1950.

White, Roberta. *A Studio of One's Own: Fictional Women Painters and the Art of Fiction.* Madison: Fairleigh Dickinson UP, 2005.

Seven Short Stories by Nancy Hale

Midsummer

⸺✸⸺

They would ride through the hot, dim woods that sultry, ominous August. From the hard ground, littered with spots of sifted sun, on the hills their horses would carry them in a minute to the hollows. There was something terrible about the hollows, deep-bottomed with decaying leaves, smelling of dead water and dark leafage and insufferable heat. The sound of the horses' feet was like a confused heartbeat on the swampy ground. They both felt it. They used to get off their horses, without having said a word, and helplessly submerge themselves in each other's arms, while the sweat ran down their backs under their shirts. They never talked there. They stood swaying together with their booted feet deep in the mulch, holding each other, hot and mystified in this green gloom. From far away in the upper meadows they could always hear the cicada reaching an unbearable, sharpened crescendo.

After a while the queer possession would grow too much for them, and, dizzy and faint, they would mount the horses again. The path carried them up to a long field where they would kick their horses and gallop wildly. The meadow grasses were dusty gold in all this heat, and when they galloped a hot wind pressed by them and all the million flies flew away from the horses' necks. Streaming and throbbing, they would pull up at the end of the field, and could laugh and begin to talk again. Dan would pull the squashed package of Camels out of the pocket of his wet blue shirt and they would each light one, with their horses' wet sides pressed together, and ride along at a walk. Then it would be time for Dan to go back to the stables to give his next lesson.

The country-club stable-yard was bright and normal, hot as thunder as they rode in, with the water in the trough near boiling and the brown horses looking out of the boxes into the sunlight. Dan put the horses away in the dark strawy stalls, and then he would walk back to Victoria, standing at the precise point where she had got off her horse. He would walk toward her in his blue shirt and brick-red breeches, his black hair mounting damp and thick from his red forehead, and his eyes as blue as an alcohol flame, lighting another of his Camels. He would offer her one. Then they would walk over to the stable-yard well and he would pull up a bucket of cold water. He would say, "Will you have some water, Miss?" and hand her some in the glass that stood on the well's edge. She looked at his shoulders and his big red throat as she drank, and pushed damp ends of hair away from her face. Then he would have a drink.

When Dan rode out of the yard again, with some group of children perched on the high horses following him, she would wave at him as he turned the corner into the road, and he would make a little bow from the neck, the bow of an Irish groom. Then he and the children would trot noisily down the macadam, Dan riding so beautifully and carelessly, half-around in his saddle, with one hand on the horse's rump, telling the children to keep their heels down. Victoria would climb into her big green roadster and drive out of the stable-yard as fast as she dared, skidding the corner and going up the road in the other direction with the ball of her foot jammed down on the accelerator.

Victoria Jesse was sixteen that sultry summer. She lived on White Hill in her parents' Italian villa with the blue tile roof, so gruesomely out of place in the New England landscape. Her parents were in France, but the servants and old Nana were in the house and the garden was kept up by the disagreeable gardener, always on his knees by the rose bushes, which dropped thick petals on the turf. The water in the cement swimming pool was soup-warm and dappled with tiny leaves from the privet bushes around. The tennis court was as hard and white as marble, and the white iron benches drawn up around its edge were so hot all day that they could not be sat upon. The Venetian blinds in the house were kept drawn, and the rooms were dim and still, with faint sweat upon the silver candlesticks and the pale marble of the hall floor.

Victoria was sixteen, and sometimes, at the end of the afternoon, when she sat in a rattan chair on the shadowed lawn, when the grass grew cooler and a breeze sprang up and the exhausted birds began to sing, she thought she would go wild with the things that were happening inside her. She wanted to stand on the edge of the pool and stretch upward until she grew taller and taller, and then dive violently into the water and never come up. She wanted to climb the huge pine tree on the lawn, throw herself upward to the top by some passionate propulsion, and stretch her arms wildly to the sky. But she could only sit around interminably in chairs on the lawn in the heat and quiet, beating with hate and awareness and bewilderment and violence, all incomprehensible to her and pulling her apart.

She could only drive her car as fast as it would go, wrenching it around corners, devouring the ribbon of road with it, driving for hours with the unformed hope of adventure; she could only be so cross with Nana and so passionately disagreeable to her old playmates on White Hill that she was not asked to play tennis or picnic, which gave her a melancholy satisfaction. She took a dizzy pleasure in going to the dances at the club with nothing on under her dress and a belt pulled tight around her waist, and dancing with the fuzzy, pink-faced boys of her age, pulsating in all her muscles to the jazz music, and then suddenly walking out and leaving as she had come, alone in her roadster, streaming along the white moonlit roads in the middle of the night, until she was so tired that she had to go home and fall into tossing sleep on the slippery white sheet of her bed.

She could not imagine what was happening to her; she had never imagined such violent sensations as beat at her; inside she was like the summer itself—sultry and fiery, and racked by instantaneous thunderstorms. At the end of the day the air relaxed into moist, nostalgic evening, but she had no relaxing, only a higher tension in the poignant secretness of night. She thought, with defiance, that she must be going crazy.

She had grown thin from her own fire and the unrelenting fire of the weather. She was white, and her green eyes burned unhappily in her pointed face; her bright, thick hair seemed thicker from being always a little damp.

Superimposed on all this ferment was the incessant preoccupation with Dan. She began to take riding lessons in June, to work off a little of this torturing energy, since she wanted to be away from the infuriating "younger crowd," and felt it might satisfy her to ride as violently as she drove a car. Dan took her out, and within half an hour, with this tropical immediacy with which she was feeling everything, she uncomprehendingly desired him and wanted to touch him, and could not take her eyes off him. She gave herself no time to be frightened at such unprecedented emotion. She got off her horse to get a drink at a deserted well in the middle of a field, and he got off to help her. With some kind of instinctive simplicity, she went and stood against him, facing him, touching him, waiting for him to do something. He acted; he put one arm around her, holding the horses' reins with the other hand, and leaned and kissed her hard. For a moment she had the first relief she had had in weeks, and from that moment she wanted him more and more to touch her and to kiss her. After his first reaction, Dan became very stilted, with a recollection of his "place" and his job, but by this time the turmoil inside her had concentrated itself on him, and she would not allow him to remount his horse or help her mount hers; she threw her arms around him with a wild relief.

He had no sophistry to combat her abandon and no way to reason or cope with her obvious passion. He had a conscientious feeling that he had no right to let her have her way, that it would be much better if he somehow put a stop to things, and he saw how young and bewildered she was. But he had never seen anybody as strange and as beautiful as she was, or had the sense of being so dangerously loved, and he saw her lack of reserve and her lack of coyness, and the vulnerability of her youth, and all his vague Irish mysticism made him respond to her as something akin to his horses and the wide countryside he loved. He had the simplicity to sense her quality of being lovely and lost, and different from the fat-legged Irish maids who were his normal social lot.

He left the extent of their relationship up to her, at first because he was impressed by the difference between their stations in life, and later because he loved her, too. He was nearly as bewildered by the queer, sultry passages between them as she was; he was nearly as lost and puzzled as she was, for different reasons. He thought she was a strange little thing, and sometimes when he lay on his mussy bed in the room off the tackroom where he slept, he felt a conceit that he was so irresistible to her, and that she had started it all; but in those submerged, lush hollows where they kissed, he was as bemused and possessed as she was.

None of it was leading to anything. Nothing in the world seemed to be leading to anything. Victoria had no idea of making Dan run away with her, or of young dreams of happiness—she was conscious only that her relief was in him. She got the nearest thing to peace in those dim hollows. The rest of her life had a fabulous, dreamy aspect to her; she lived through these days minute by minute.

One evening she had a telegram from her parents. She was having strawberries for dessert, and sitting limply at the end of the table while two white candles flickered in the wind from the west window. Her fresh yellow dress clung slightly to her shoulders, and her hair felt heavy. The telegram said that they would be home the next day.

She heard the mail plane to New York muttering its way through the evening sky. She heard the servants talking and rattling the dishes out in the kitchen. As long as she might live, she could never forget the immediacy of the streaky pink strawberries and cream before her, the wan look of white wax trickling down the candles, and the little wind stirring in the short hair at the back of her neck.

She got up and opened the door that led out into the garden, and all the renewed scents of evening flowed in like sweet liquors. She walked out on the grass and the dew wet her stockings above the tops of her slippers. The vicious sweetness of the summer night was intolerable and she leaned against a lilac tree, thinking, What is going to become of me? What is all this beauty and this desire that I cannot touch or take within my hand, and what shall I do? They will try to take me back, and I will never be happy again. What shall I *do*? Oh my God, what is the matter with me? Why do these desires for I don't know what run through me like hot and cold? I don't want to see my mother and father. I couldn't face them, because I am not their child any more, I am nobody at all, I have become only these desperate desires that drive me wild. Why am I so lost?

Her mind went round and round and helped her no more than ever, but seemed to be submerged by the smells, the touch of bark under her fingers, and the taste of flowers on the air. As usual, her vague desperation resolved itself in a need for action, and she went out to the drive and got into her car, whose seat was wet with mist. She roared out into the road and down through the town and tore out along the country roads. The bobbing glare of the headlights showed up the leaves of the branches that hung over the road, and the white road, and the grass along the edges. Outside this, the night was immense and breathing and terrible. She could only cut a white hole through it. She had worn no hat, and the wind scraped her temples and raked her hair.

She drove for two hours as fast as she could, at the end finding herself headed for the stables and Dan. As she turned in the drive into the stable-yard, she thought, How ridiculous! I must have known I was coming here. Why didn't I come at once? She stopped the car and went around to the back, where the little room off the tackroom had a light in its window.

She knocked, and Dan came and let her in. He was surprised and very much embarrassed. He was dressed in his riding things, but he had taken his boots off and his breeches fitted to his bare white legs. She came in and sat down on his narrow bed. Several moths whacked against the chimney of the oil lamp. Dan had been reading the *Rider & Driver*, and it lay on the bare floor with his boots.

"You mustn't be here, Miss," he said. "It's not the place for you to be coming."

"My family's getting back tomorrow," she said.

"Will you have a cigarette?" He held his crumpled package of Camels out to her. Their little ceremony of lighting took place, with them looking at each other over the flame, solemnly.

They sat and smoked. There had never been any real attempt at verbal communication between them, and now they said nothing at all, but sat by the oil lamp and listened to the sawing of the crickets in the marshes outside. Far away somewhere, someone was playing a harmonica.

She made no reply to his telling her that she should not be there, and he said nothing about her family's return. They both forgot. They looked at each other gravely, with concentration, and said nothing.

"What am I going to do, Dan?" she asked after a long time.

"I dunno."

"What is life all about?" she asked, not really caring about an answer.

"I dunno," he said again. "I like the horses, but I dunno, if you mean about dyin' and all." His face was beautiful and simple, cut in the sharp, lovely planes of the Irish.

She had nothing to talk to him about, really. She wanted to be with him. She felt a relief now, she was almost perfectly happy, in a dazed, numb way. They simply stared at each other for a long time. She could not take her eyes from his face. All the wild, furious bewilderment in her seemed to leave her as she looked at him, and she felt she wanted to go on looking forever. Then the lamp flickered and faded. Dan got up and turned it up. The queer magic broke like an eggshell.

There was a lot she could have begun to talk about—her family, and what he and she were going to do about seeing each other when they returned, and a dozen other thoughts in the back of her mind—but she felt no real desire to.

"I wish I could stay here with you," she said, breaking the long silence.

"Ah, you couldn't do that, Miss," he said.

He came back to the bed where she sat, and sat down stiffly beside her. She lay down and pulled him down beside her. It was the first time that they had ever lain side by side. She felt calm and peaceful.

"My little darling," he mumbled suddenly into her hair. He had his arms quietly around her.

"Oh, Dan, I love you so."

After that they did not speak. They did not move. They both lay in drowsy stillness. She was plunged into a dreamless daze, wanting nothing, in a deep well of content. He felt the same strange, unreal sense of peace. Neither of them thought at all.

Finally they slept, with their cheeks together. The lamp went out after a while, and soon pale day streaked along the floor through the little window. Victoria got up, and Dan stood up too, and they moved and stretched themselves without saying anything. He threw open the door, and the fresh smells of the morning flooded the close air. On the other side of the wall, they could hear the horses champing and moving their feet.

They went out into the stable-yard. Hens were making a lot of noise and some birds flew low to the ground. The green car stood there in the early mist, bulky and practical. Victoria got in and closed the door. It made a heavy, solid sound. Dan stood beside the car and they looked at each other for a moment, vaguely. Then she drove slowly out of the yard. He walked back to his room, still in his bare feet, with the breeches-ends about his calves. Victoria drove home along the country roads as it grew lighter, and threw herself into bed and was instantly asleep.

She did not wake until eleven, and then Mr. and Mrs. Jesse had returned and were waiting to have it out with her. They had had four letters from fellow-townsmen informing them that their daughter was carrying on with the riding instructor at the club, a common Irishman. The Jesses were the richest people in the town, and before Victoria was even awake they had arranged that Dan should be discharged immediately, with wages in advance. The club steward was having him packed off on the noon train. They had done everything they could. Now there was nothing left but the talk with Victoria.

They sat in the dim library, and she came in to them. The heat was already at its height. They talked and talked. They told her how common such an affair was, over and over. They tried to find out just how much she had actually done. They were furious and hurt and outraged.

Nothing they said made any impression on Victoria. She heard their voices far, far away, and she got a sort of detached impression of what they were saying. She sat in a big chair, languidly, while her dress wilted and clung around her, and watched the leaves outside make the light flicker between the slits of the Venetian blinds.

Finally, bewildered at her detachment, they told her that the instructor had already left, had been fired for his conduct. They told her four times before she understood what they were talking about. She looked at them vaguely and without saying anything for a few minutes, and then fainted and could not be brought to for some time.

Dr. Russell, with his little mustache and long tubes of colored pills, told them it was the logical result of the protracted heat wave. She was as thin as a bag of bones, and as white as a sheet, and gave every sign of physical and nervous exhaustion. He prescribed two tonics, and said she must stay in bed for a day or two.

She lay in bed all afternoon, trying to concentrate. She couldn't get anything straight in her head. She would remember that Dan had gone, and then she would remember that she loved Dan, but by that time she had forgotten that he had left, and it was impossible for her to assemble things to make any picture of what her life was. She was not very unhappy. She was hot and tired, and the only things she could think about without an effort were the somber hollows where she and Dan had gone, with their curious green gloom and the smell of submerged decay. Her mind rested in those hollows, dim and steaming.

Her mother came in to see her late in the afternoon, with a plate of strawberries for her. She sat down on the edge of the bed and kissed Victoria gently.

"Darling," she said. "Poor little child. I shall never forgive myself for leaving you alone this summer. You mustn't be too unhappy. Daddy understands and I understand, and we want you to rest and be our happy little girl again. It's really our fault that you fell into the power of this dreadful man."

"He isn't a dreadful man," Victoria said, and closed her mouth tight. It was an effort to talk. She turned her face aside and pretended to go to sleep. After a while her mother went away, leaving the strawberries by the side of the bed. Victoria turned over and looked at them lying on the white plate.

It grew dusky in her room, and then it grew dark. The little breeze of the evening came faltering through the window. Victoria got up and went to the window and breathed the terrible sweetness of the garden at night.

In her nightgown, she climbed down the honeysuckle trellis below her window, and dropped to the grass. She had used the trellis for running away when she was small, and she stood at the foot and thought about that for a while, how impossible that that small girl was the same as herself now. She gave it up.

Barefooted, she walked along the terrace to the lilac tree where she had stood last night, and stood there again, swaying a little, remembrances and thoughts swirling in her head.

Suddenly she pulled her nightgown off over her head and threw herself down on the wet turf. The smell of it filled her nostrils. She pressed her body violently against its softness and fragrance, and ran her fingers desperately into the damp earth. Dan, Dan had gone and all her heart had gone, too. Everything had gone. If life was to be as terrible, progressively, as it had come to be at sixteen, she wished she might die now. She wished she were dead, and felt the exquisite touch of dew-soaked grass against her breast.

1934

The Empress's Ring

⏤⏤∽∾∽⏤⏤

I worry about it still, even today, thirty-odd years
later. I close my eyes to go to sleep at night, sometimes, and I am back at the old, disintegrated sand pile where
I lost it, digging in the dirt-mixed sand with my fingernails to
find my little ring.

It was tiny, a little girl's ring that was said to have belonged
to the Empress of Austria. I suppose that would have been Elisabeth, the beautiful one who climbed mountains. It was given
to me, I think on my eighth birthday, by a family friend whom
I called Aunt and who was herself so erect, so blond, so high-
voiced that I thought of her privately as a princess. I was told
that she had bought the ring in an auction room in Vienna and
brought it home—all for me.

The ring was gold, with a curly banner across the top which
was set with five little turquoises. The gold setting of the stones
was etched or engraved; it gave a delicate and lacy effect. I
thought it was the most beautiful ring, the most royal ring.

"Far too good for a child to wear," my nurse said firmly. I can see her entwining her fat red fingers as she said it. "You won't be wearing it out to play, that's one thing."

But the thing was that I did. I was compelled to after her saying that. For nobody—certainly not she—could understand the love I had for that ring, and the absolute impossibility of my ever losing anything so precious. I wore it when I went out to play in the shed that adjoined the old barn and connected it with the abandoned milkhouse that was now called my playhouse.

Getting a playhouse, even a makeshift one, had been a sort of victory a little while back. Our only neighbors, the Wilkinsons, had a daughter named Mimi, who had a real playhouse, one built for the purpose: a tiny model of a cottage, with little green shutters at the windows, a shingled roof, a door with a shiny brass knocker engraved "Mimi," and, inside, miniature chairs and a table upon which Mimi, a girl with natural ringlets, set out tea parties with real Dresden china made for children's use, china with pink rosebuds which were unendurably thrilling—pink rosebuds and gold rims.

Ours was not the place for that kind of thing at all. We had nothing that was modern, nothing that was fascinating like rosebuds on little new china teacups. Our big white house seemed to settle down deeper into the ground with every spring freshet. The barn was red. The place had once been a working farm, but all that was left of that now was the stanchions in the lower barn; the horse stalls in the upper barn, where one could stand and look out of the little horse windows over the swamp at the melancholy woods beyond and imagine that one was a horse; the market garden of rhubarb that came up doggedly year after year, no matter how many boxes of furnace ashes were dumped upon it (the rhubarb ended by coming up out of the ground at least six feet higher than the original garden had been); and the little house at the end of the woodshed, which had once been used to prepare the milk for marketing. There was a sort of slot at the front of this milkhouse, and the cans had been shoved out through it into a big box with a lid, where they could be picked up by the men who took them away. But of this I had only been told. Now there was no activity on our place. The pines in front of the house sighed and whistled in winter, the dandelions came up like little suns all over the lawns in springtime, the swamp turned from gold to crimson to purple as the summer passed sadly by, and in autumn the pumpkins lay rotting on the ground down below the lower barn.

I had to have a playhouse. I wept. And so the abandoned milkhouse was swept out, some of my nursery furniture was moved into it, and an ornate Victorian knocker was screwed on to the weathered board door that would not quite close, and it was officially referred to as my playhouse.

What was it that was wrong? It was not really a playhouse, to begin with—but I had imagined far wilder excursions than this required. I made the effort; I imagined that the too high shelves inside, where cans had been stacked, were really shelves for my own needs, to put books and toys and tea-party china on. I imagined that the bulkhead which contained the slot for pushing out the cans was really a window seat.

My mother gave me some china to use for my own efforts at tea parties. Rosebuds were what I yearned for, rosebuds were what I dreamed about at night. Small, neat rosebuds on a field of glistening milk-white china—little china, made for children. What I got was probably much nicer. It was the odds and ends of an old broken-up adult tea set—orange-and-white china with gold arabesques. I set it on the too high shelves—the plates on edge against the wall, the teacups in a row, the saucers in a pile, the teapot turned so that the broken spout did not show. It was probably very beautiful. But there was nothing, there could have been nothing, that would take the place of pink rosebuds.

Then I was given my little blue ring. It was a ring meant for a little girl to wear. It was real gold, and real turquoises. It was beautiful, and it had belonged to an empress.

It belonged to my hand. It was just the right size. In the morning sun, when I went out to play, its five turquoises shone in a curly row. Even all those years later, I can remember looking at it and feeling satisfied, complete, and happy.

It was probably not the first day I wore it that I lost it, but I did not have it very long. I went to play in the old sand pile that moldered away in the inner corner of the shed nearest to the barn. The sand pile was the remains of several cartloads of sand that had been dumped there, but since there was no frame to hold the sand (such as Mimi's sand pile had) it had sifted, filtered away, become mixed with the dirt of the woodshed, disintegrated, spread out; it was another of the things I had that had something the matter with them.

I don't know why I went to play in the sand pile at all. I was too old, and this was my playhouse stage. But sometimes I did go and play in it, in the scattered remains of my babyhood, just as sometimes I went and slid into the hole under the foundations of the barn that I had discovered when I was four—not to hide any more, not for any game, just to be in there and feel it around me again.

I went to the sand pile again, at the wrong age, and, whether the first time or a later one, I lost my little ring playing in it. The loss did not strike me all at once.

I came in to lunch, and my nurse said, "There. Will you look? You've lost your beautiful gold ring with the stones in it, just as I told you you would."

I said nothing. I looked at my horribly bare hand and looked back at her, not showing anything. I didn't want her to see anything. Because I was convinced that it was because she had told me that I would lose my precious possession if I wore it out to play that I had lost it. I didn't want her to know this.

"I know *exactly* where it is," I said. "It's not lost at all."

And in a way I did know exactly where it was. It was in the sand pile somewhere, and the sand pile was not more than ten feet wide, even in its disintegrated condition. It had to be there. I looked and looked—that day and other days, too—with a hollow, painful feeling inside me because I had lost my precious possession. At some point, I must have given up.

But I never completely gave up, because years later, in my teens, I would suddenly remember my ring, the one I had lost, and would go out to the sand pile, by now almost obliterated but still a definite area to me, and dig and dig. It had to be there. I never found it, but it was there just the same, somewhere in the mingled sand and dirt, within a definite space about ten feet square.

Once, I dreamed that I had found it. It was when I was a young girl going to dances, and the dream was about the most irrelevant to my life that could be imagined. But when I woke, with the clear memory of finding the ring and seeing it lie in my palm with its banner of five little blue stones, my excitement and the verisimilitude were so great that I went out to the woodshed—in a beige crêpe-de-Chine dress, I remember, that reached my knees; high heels, and my hair shingled—and began to dig once again. Then the telephone rang for me, or someone drove up in a car. But after the dream it was not finding it that seemed unbelievable.

Even now, in another part of the country, I sometimes remember my ring and wonder why I could never find it. Today, for example, I took a walk in this Southern springtime, filled with the sound of the persistent mourning dove and the occasional trill of the wood thrush. I passed the brook, which is called a run, and the thicket of bamboos that grows beside it, and mounted the gentle rise that leads on past the Lambeths' house. The Lambeths have a lovely house—old, built of pink brick, but all made fresh, all charming and inviting; inside, their floors gleam, their chintzes are trimly fitted to the chairs, and they drink their whiskey out of silver tumblers with gadroon edges. I would love tumblers like that, but they must cost a fortune. As I rounded the curve just before the entrance to the Lambeths' house, I thought I would stop and pay them a call. It would be fun to sit before their crackling fire and drink their whiskey from one of those enchanting tumblers, and perhaps come to know them better. But as I came abreast of the drive, I saw that two cars were parked near the door. The Lambeths already had callers. I felt a little hollow and passed on.

When I made the circuit that brought me home, I felt thirsty and got myself a drink of water. My glasses are a sorry collection, the odds and ends of a number of broken sets. I went upstairs then and into my room, where I tidied up a little before lying down to take a nap. I don't know why it is that Mrs. Hildreth, who makes my slipcovers, can never make the arms fit properly; the cording lies unevenly upon the frame of the chair and gives a sloppy appearance.

I lay down, and as soon as I closed my eyes, there I was again, years and years later, back in the old woodshed of the place where I grew up, scratching and clawing at the sand pile, trying to find my little blue ring. I'm sure there is not as much sand, nearly, left there any more as I see when I close my eyes. There may not be any sand at all; the place is sold, and the new owners may have fixed everything up, torn down the shed, perhaps even put up a new, properly fenced-in sand pile somewhere for their growing children. I don't know.

Perhaps if the old sand pile is still there, one of the new owner's children will one day really find my ring, for it is there somewhere. Perhaps the child—a little girl—will be poking about with a tin shovel and will turn up that scrap of gold with its five little blue stones. I wonder what she will make of it.

1954

Entrance Into Life

—◦◦◦—

*A*s the little boy and his mother walked up the brick-paved hill from the university hospital, the crowds were gathering. Young men hurried by with their gowns fluttering about their legs, carrying their tasseled caps under their arms. Up on the lawn the people stood about in their summer clothes in the afternoon sunshine, talking and laughing and waiting for the procession to start down to the amphitheatre. A brass band was playing out in the middle of the lawn.

Robert kept close hold of his mother's hand as they joined the crowds and went and stood by a white column in the shade. As soon as they stopped walking and stood still, he began to cough again. After the coughing was all over he opened his eyes, and the sun was still shining and the people were wandering slowly across the grass and along the colonnade and he could hear the band.

His hand that Mary, his mother, held was very thin and small. She squeezed it and looked down at him and smiled when he finished coughing. He looked so neat and small and clean in his white shirt and his little brown shorts. His hair was smoothed down with water.

He was six years old. He had a fox terrier for a pet, and he had had two friends in his life, a boy named Llewellyn and a girl named Polly. Last Christmas he had made a picture for his mother for a Christmas present, of a round, yellow moon over a red barn. He could read a little bit.

"Now what are we going to do?" he asked.

"We're going to watch all the boys march down the lawn to graduate," she said. "They've been at college for the past few years and now they're going to get their diplomas and go out into the world to make their fortunes."

"What did they take the pictures for?" he asked.

"The pictures? Oh, they were pictures to see if there were any little spots on your lungs."

"What will we do if there are any little spots?"

"We'll just do things to make the little spots go away again," she said, and looked away from his small, interested white face.

Among the crowds of people—young, pretty girls in shady hats, and mothers, and fathers—there were a great many children running about underfoot all over the lawn. They threaded in and out through the crowds, and threw themselves down on the grass and rolled, and went and stood staring in a circle around the brass band. Mary hoped Robert would not want to go and run with them.

"That music they're playing is 'The Merry Widow'," she said. "I love it, don't you? . . . They're all going to graduate."

"Did Daddy graduate here?"

"Yes. And I came and watched him and it was just like this that you're seeing now. I had on a pink dress and a big black hat. And Daddy marched down the lawn with all the other boys, just the way you're going to see them do in a minute."

Now the band had begun to play "The Stars and Stripes Forever" and all was brave and sunny with the crowds and the laughter: the girls with red hair and yellow hair, with little thin waists and light dresses, and all the mothers, talking to their sons, who stood braced to break away and join the procession in their caps and gowns, and said, "Yes, Mother. Unh-hunh. You bet." There was an air of triumph on the lawn, and of something accomplished, and of celebration, crowned with the music of the band.

Now the crowds in black, on the steps of the Rotunda, began to take shape into a double file, and down the steps came the marshal, in scarlet and dark blue. The people on the lawn hurried to the center to line the procession as it came slowly, slowly, down. Mary found a place where she could see and held Robert in front of her, with a hand on each of his shoulders. The band was playing the "March of the Priests."

They came on and on, more of them, hundreds of them, all the young men, with their gowns flapping about their long legs, with their faces red in the sunshine, with their strong necks rising from the collars of their gowns. There were short boys and tall boys, thin ones and fat, with faces looking straight ahead. Mary saw one boy bring a Mason jar out from under his gown and take a swallow from it, still without moving his eyes from a point directly before him. There were more and more, all the young men who had been to college.

Every year in June there would be as many more, and there had been for all the Junes going back, except during the confusion of the war years. Mary kept remembering how she had stood here and watched Harry go by, and how they had been to the dances for three nights before and were going to the Final Ball that night.

She had tears in her eyes. It was like a wedding, the ending to something. All the young men came marching past, who had grown up and done with schools, who had gone to war and come back, who had played football and listened to lectures and got drunk and now were going to start living, somehow, beyond the commitments and the regulations of children. In whatever world, they were grown up now. The band played, and the procession passed slowly across the lawn, and the crowds, watching, broke up and followed it down to the amphitheatre for the exercises there.

Robert and his mother were left standing alone on the grass.

"Aren't we going down there too?" he asked.

"No," Mary said. "We'd better go on home now. The graduation will take a long time. They have to hand out diplomas to all those hundreds of boys."

"What's diplomas?"

"A piece of paper that says each boy has done all the work he's supposed to and passed his examinations."

They started to walk, hand in hand, away from the crowds, back to where the car was parked. At the end of the lawn, Robert began to cough, and they stood still until he had stopped. He wiped his eyes with his clean white handkerchief. Then he took his mother's hand again and they walked on.

"Did Daddy get a diploma?"

"Yes, he did. He was very important, too. He was the secretary of his class and he played on the football team. When I used to come to the dances here, he was the handsomest boy in college."

"Will I go to this college?" Robert said.

She looked down at his small, white face.

When he was first born she had used to look in his scrap of a face to see a boy's face there and what it would be like.

Now she was looking for a young man's face, a college boy's, one facing a grownup world, of whatever kind. She shut her eyes because she could not find any such face; inside her eyes everything was dark gray and cold, and all at once it might have been the middle of winter. She did not know where to begin to look for spring.

But when she opened her eyes the sun was still shining.

"Yes, darling," she said. "All your Daddy's family went here."

"Will you come and see me when I graduate?"

"Of course I will," she said. "Of course I will."

And from far away they could hear the brass band still playing bravely and triumphantly in the sunny afternoon.

1947

The Earliest Dreams

⸻

I

*T*hat was long, long ago.

Your bed was maple, the color of brown sugar, and upon the small round posts of it in the darkness some moonlight danced in the hush, in the quiet. Your mother had rustled away, far away and bright and legendary, and your window stood open to the great stars and the wide dark snow. It was so quiet, and the air of the night and the snow came through the window and smelled so cold, so sweet, and of faraway sad promises. What was it you wanted so? From miles and miles away you heard a late train breathing across the countryside, hurrying distantly through the white winter night to the yellow lights and the little quiet towns. Its whistle blew, so far far away, three times, Ah, Ah, Aaaah…. You longed for something, lying still between two smooth slices of sheet, but you could not think what it was, and now you will never know what it was.

Downstairs they were all laughing in the dining room, and you could hear both the two sounds, the waves of cool mythical laughter underneath your room, and from the back of the house, coming up the back stairs, the comfortable low clatter in the kitchen. Bridie and Catherine, moving about in the hot yellow light in the kitchen, over the dry brown boards of the floor, between the white table and the sink, between the pantry with all the cups on hooks, the bags of flour and the crocks of potatoes and the jugs of molasses and vinegar that stood in a black cupboard under the marble slab, up a little creaking step to the stove. You thought of the stove, as black as your hat with strange wonderful things to eat steaming in covered pots, and the piles of plates heating up on the shelf at the back. You could hear the footsteps heavy and busy across the old boards, and your heart caught in your throat when they opened the door to go in to wait on the dinner-party and all the laughter came upstairs suddenly in a gust.

Outside the house a car drove by up the dark road, with a broken chain around its wheel, rapping as fast and muffled as a heartbeat upon the frozen snow, louder and louder, and the lights came in the window and ran along the wall until they came to the bed. For just a minute your bed was blue-white and bright, and then the lights scraped along the other wall, bobbing up and down along the pictures and over the book-case, and ran out of the window so fast. Far up the road the broken chain beat on the snow on the road, further and further and then it was gone away. It was enormous and still outside, deep in the breathing snow, with the stars a million miles deep in the high sky.

They were laughing downstairs. It rang like bells, like the wind running in and out among little bells, fewer and fewer and then all at once another and another until the bells were all tinkling and singing in different keys. You heard the important clatter of plates, fragile, impossible, fairy plates. What were they all laughing at? Something you knew nothing about, something beautiful and exalted. You wondered why they always laughed so much in the evenings after you had gone to bed. In the lovely evenings, in the pale candle-light shut in from the white night, they were all so beautiful downstairs in their dresses and their little colored slippers. They knew about strange things, places, and shining people, great singers and dancers from Russia, balls in Vienna and cities in China, and they knew slender little jokes that nobody but they could understand. You never knew what they were laughing at when they laughed so long in the evenings.

II

You lay very still in your bed and listened to something, perhaps a dead leaf, perhaps a twig from the top of the house, fall with the gentlest pat upon the surface of the vast, murmurous snow. Forever, all over the round smooth world it was dark and still and beautifully cold, fatefully and eternally hushed; under you only was a house full of lights and the sound of people laughing. Lying there you felt yourself rising higher and higher into the dark sky where the stars shone; where the stars burned like heavenly secrets, high and coldly radiant.

You were suspended in a dark tower above the world. Planets and great winds, chimeras and islands lost under the sea, and archangels striding among the stars. And a great bell tolling.

You heard the peal of the front-doorbell sing through the house, and someone opened a door and all the laughter came up to you in a clear sudden burst. And then they closed the door, somewhere, and the sound clapped shut, and you could hear them laughing faintly, far away.

You thought about the little animals in the woods beyond the snow, the rabbits packed together in warm clusters in holes, and little mice among the roots of trees. You thought about the unheard fall of cold leaves at intervals, among the trees upon the drifted snow. You thought of the silent woods, where there were no lights and no sound, with perhaps the infinitely small track of an animal running momentarily under the trees in the dark. Beyond lay the meadows rolling over the hills, with the moon shining blank white and pure upon the snow, with the wind sliding like a skimmer over the crust, and the great stars in the sky above the world.

You held the pillow up to your face and fitted it to your cheek, and lay still in the room you knew so well. You alone were alive in this still, unbelievable world, in your own room with its long window.

The moonlight lay along the glass of the pictures and across the bookcase, and you thought about the books in their shelves and the three white chairs and the black table and your desk, all ranged in the darkness around you.

III

Then downstairs someone began to play the piano, and you listened to the muted music. What was it that you did not know about, what was it that you wanted? You knew there was something that the music had known and wept for, something that was over and could never be forgotten, but for you it had never been begun. You felt so sad, so happy and so sad, because something that was all the beauty and the tears in the world was over, that something lovely was lost and could only be remembered, and still you knew that for you the thing had not yet started. Perhaps you were sad for the regret you knew you would feel someday for this sadness. The music was bitter and sweet and sorrowfully reckless, very fast and resigned and gay in a minor key. You wondered what it was that had made the music so sad, that made you so sad.

Then they stopped playing and it was all still again. The moon moved as slow as a cloud into the frame of your window, and stood still in the sky outside, and you lay in your bed in the dark and watched the moon. Outdoors the quiet snow and the sky beat like a pulse, and then you heard a leaf scrambling across the crust of the snow, scratching minutely with fingers of wire; it slid, and ceased.

They were all laughing in the drawing room below. You wondered what they were laughing at, that made the laughter sound so wise, so gay, so confident and foreign. You never knew what things they laughed at when they laughed so long in the evenings, and now you never will know.

1934

The Bubble

———∞∞∞———

*N*ow when Eric was born in Washington, D.C., I was eighteen, and most people thought I was too young to be having a baby.

I went down there two months before it was going to come, to stay at my mother-in-law's house. She was crazy for the baby to be born in Washington, and I was just as glad to get away from New York. My father had been divorced from my mother, and she had gone abroad, and he was getting married to Estrella, so I couldn't go *there*, and I had got so I couldn't stand that first awful little apartment, with the ivory woodwork and a red sateen sofa; I didn't know how to make it look attractive, and it depressed me. Tom, Eric's father, stayed on in it after I went to his mother's; I remember he used to work in a bond house.

It felt strange, staying with my mother-in-law. She had a big house, right opposite to the old British Embassy. That makes you realize how long ago this was, and yet I am still, all these years later, wondering about why it was the way it was. Mrs. Tompkins' house was a real house, with five stories and four servants, and meals at regular times and a gong that the colored butler rang to call you to them. I had never lived in a real house. My father always had apartments with day beds in them, so we could open the whole place up to parties, and we ate any time. My father was an art critic on the *Tribune*. Nobody remembers who he was any more; everybody forgets things so fast.

My room in Washington was in the front, on the top floor, looking out at the rambling, old, mustard-yellow Embassy. Sometimes at night I would lean on the window sill and watch the cars draw up and the people in evening dress get out and walk up the strip of crimson carpet they rolled out across the sidewalk for the Embassy parties. And I would weep, up there on the fourth floor, because I was so big and clumsy, and I felt as if I would never, never go dancing again, or walk along a red carpet, or wear a low-cut dress. The last time I had was one night when I went dancing at the old Montmartre with Tom and Eugene—I was in love with Eugene—and I had seen myself in a long mirror dancing and realized how fat I looked, and that was another reason I wanted to get away from New York and go and have it in Washington. I had two black dresses—one plain wool and the other with an accordion-pleated crêpe skirt—and one velour hat, and I wore them and wore them and wore them all those last weeks, and I swore to myself that when it was born I would burn them in the fireplace in my room there. But I never did.

I used to live in a kind of fever for the future, when the baby would come and I would look nice again and go back to New York and see Eugene. I took regular walks along the Washington streets—N Street, and Sixteenth Street, and Connecticut Avenue with all the attractive people going into restaurants to lunch—in my shapeless black dress and my velour hat, dreaming of the day when I would be size 12 and my hair would curl again and I would begin to have fun. All those days before Eric was born were aimed frontward, hard; I was just getting through them for what it would be like afterward. My mother-in-law was the one who was really having the baby; she was full of excitement about it, and used to take me to Washington shops to buy baby clothes. Looking back all these years later, I remember those sunny afternoons in late winter, and the little white dresses and embroidered caps and pink sweaters spread out on the counter, and stopping to have tea and cinnamon toast at the Mayflower, with the small orchestra playing hotel music, and they seem beautiful and tranquil, but in those days I was doing any old thing she suggested, and I was living to get back to New York and begin having fun again.

I remember she gave a ladies' luncheon for me, to meet some of the young mothers she thought I would like to know. I suppose they were a couple of years older than I, but they seemed middle-aged to me and interested in the stupidest things; I wanted to cry because nobody was anything like me.

But now I remember that the luncheon was really beautiful. The dining room was big and long, and on the sideboard was Mrs. Tompkins' silver *repoussé* tea service. The table was laid with a huge white damask cloth, and the napkins had lace inserts. It was a real ladies' lunch party, with twelve ladies and a five-course luncheon; I had never been to one before in my life, and I seldom have since. I remember the first course was shrimp cocktails in glasses set in bowls filled with crushed ice. And for dessert there was a special confection, which had been ordered from Demonet's, the famous Washington caterer; it was a monument of cake and ice cream and whipped cream and cherries and angelica. But all I could think about was how food bored me and how I wanted to get back and begin living again. I felt in such a hurry.

Later that day, Mrs. Tompkins gave me a lot of her linens. It was before dinner. We used to sit in the small library and listen to Amos and Andy every night at seven. And this night she brought in a great armful of linens to show me, and everything I admired she would give me. There were damask tablecloths with borders of iris and borders of the Greek key, and round embroidered linen tea cloths, and dozens and dozens of lace and net doilies to go under finger bowls, and towels of the finest huck with great padded monograms embroidered on them. "Dear child," she said, "I want for you to have everything nice." I ended up with a whole pile of things. I wonder what ever became of them. I remember imagining what my father would have thought if he could have seen me with a lot of tablecloths and towels in my lap. "The purchase money of the Philistines," he might have said. But I have no idea what happened to all that linen, and my father is dead long ago and nobody remembers him any more. I remember when I went up to my room to change into my other dress for dinner I wept, because I was so big and ugly and all surrounded with lace doilies and baby clothes and Eugene might fall in love with somebody else before I could get back to New York.

That was the night the baby started to come.

It began about ten o'clock, just before bedtime, and when I told my mother-in-law her face lit up. She went and telephoned to the doctor and to the nurse, and then came back and told me the doctor said I was to rest quietly at home until the pains started to come every fifteen minutes, and that the nurse, Miss Hammond, would be right over. I went up to my room and lay down. It didn't hurt too much. When Miss Hammond arrived, she stood by my bed and smiled at me as if I were wonderful. She was tall and thin with sallow hair, an old-maid type.

About one o'clock, Mrs. Tompkins telephoned the doctor again, and he said to take me to the hospital. Mrs. Tompkins told me she had wired Tom to take the midnight down, but I didn't care; I was having pains regularly, and the difference had begun, the thing I have always wondered about.

We all got in a taxi, Mrs. Tompkins and Miss Hammond and I, there in the middle of the night, and drove through the dark Washington streets to the hospital. It was portentous, that drive, significant; every minute, I mean every present minute, seemed to matter. I had stopped living ahead, the way I had been doing, and was living in right now. That is what I am talking about.

I hadn't worn my wedding ring since I fell in love with Eugene. I'd told my mother-in-law that I didn't like the feeling of a ring, which was true. But in the taxi, in the darkness, she took off her own wedding ring and put it on my finger. "Dear child," she said, "I just won't have you going to the hospital with no ring." I remember I squeezed her hand.

I was taken at once to my room in the hospital, where they "prepared" me, and then almost immediately to the delivery room, because they thought the baby was coming right away. But then the pains slowed down, and I stayed in the delivery room for a long time, until the sun began to stream through the east window. The doctor, a pleasant old man with a Southern accent, had come, and he sat in the sunshine reading the morning newspaper. As I lay on my back on the high, narrow delivery cot, the pains got steadily harder, but I remember thinking, There's nothing scary about this. It just feels natural. The pains got harder and harder.

There was the doctor, and a nurse, and my own Miss Hammond, whom I felt I had known forever; occasionally she would wipe my forehead with a cool, wet cloth. I felt gay and talkative. I said, "I know what this pain feels like. It feels as if I were in a dark tunnel that was too small for me, and I were trying to squeeze through it to get to the end, where I can see a little light."

The doctor laughed. "That's not what you're doin'," he said. "That's what the baby's doin.'"

But that was the way it felt, all the same.

"Let me know when you need a little somethin'," he said.

After a while I said, "This is *bad*." And instantly he was at my side with a hypodermic needle, which he thrust into my arm, and the pain was blunted for a time.

"Let me know when you need a little somethin'," he said again.

But I was feeling very strong and full of power. I was working my way down that long, dark tunnel that was too tight for me, down toward the little light that showed at the far end. Then I had a terrible pain. That's all I'm going to stand, I thought calmly. Deliberately I opened my mouth and screamed.

At once, they put a mask over my face, and the doctor's voice said, "Breathe deeply."

And I was out.

I would come back into the brilliant sunshine of the room and the circle of faces around me, and smile up at them, and they would smile back. And then a fresh pain would approach, and I would say, "Now."

"Bear down," the doctor's voice said as the mask covered my face and I faded away from the room. "Bear down."

So I would bear down, and be gone.

Back in the sunny room and out again, several times, I went. And then, on one of the returns, to my astonishment, I heard a small, high wail that I nevertheless knew all about. Over to one side of me stood a crib on stilts; it had been standing there all along, but now above its edge I could see two tiny blue things waving faintly.

"It's a boy," I heard my darling Miss Hammond's voice saying. "You've got a beautiful boy, Mrs. Tompkins."

And then I felt a fearful pain coming. They put the mask over my face for the last time, and I went completely out.

When I woke up, it was in my own room. Mrs. Tompkins was there, and Miss Hammond, and Tom. They kissed me, and beamed at me, and Tom kept pressing my hand. But I was immune from them all.

I was inwardly enthroned. Seated on a chair of silver, sword in hand, I was Joan of Arc. I smiled at them all, because I might as well, but I needed nobody, nothing. I was the meaning of achievement, here, now, in the moment, and the afternoon sun shone proudly in from the west.

A nurse entered bearing a pale-blue bundle and put it in my arms. It was Eric, of course, and I looked down into his minute face with a feeling of old familiarity. Here he was. Here we were. We were everything.

"Your father's come," Mrs. Tompkins said.

My father's head appeared round the door, and then he came in, looking wry, as he did when people not his kind were around. He leaned down to kiss me.

"Brave girl," he whispered. "You fooled 'em."

That was right. I had fooled them, fooled everybody. I had the victory, and it was here and now.

Then the nurse took the baby away, and Miss Hammond brought a big tray of food and cranked my bed up for me to eat it. I ate an enormous dinner, and then fell asleep and did not wake up for fifteen hours.

When I woke, it was the middle of the night, and the hospital was silent around me. Then, faintly, from somewhere down the corridor, although the month was February, someone began to sing "Silent Night." It was eerie, in my closed room, to hear singing in the darkness. I looked at where the window showed pale gray and oblong. Then I realized what the tune was that was being sung, and felt horribly embarrasscd. I could hear my father saying, "These good folk with their sentimental religiosity." Then the sound of the singing disappeared, and I was never sure where it had come from, or, indeed, whether I had really heard it or not.

Next morning, bright and early, a short, thin man with gray curly hair walked into my hospital room and said, "What's all this nonsense about your not wanting to nurse your baby? I won't have it. You *must* nurse your child." He was the pediatrician, Dr. Lawford.

Nobody had ever given me an order before. My father believed in treating me as if I were grown-up. I stared at the strange man seating himself by the window, and burst into tears.

"I tell you what, my dear little girl," he said after a few moments. "I'll make a bargain with you. I believe you have to go back to New York and take up your life in six weeks. Nurse your baby until you have to go, and then you can wean him."

I nodded. I didn't know anything about any of it—only what older women said to me, about nursing ruining your figure—and all of that seemed in another life now.

Flowers began to arrive, great baskets of them from all Mrs. Tompkins' friends, and they filled my room until it looked like a bower. Telegrams arrived. A wire came, late one day, from Eugene. It read, "Aren't You Something." But Eugene no longer seemed quite real, either.

I would lie in that hospital bed with the baby within my arm, nursing him. I remember it with Dr. Lawford sitting in the chair by the window and tall, old-maidish Miss Hammond standing beside my bed, both of them watching me with indulgent faces. I felt as though they were my father and my mother, and I their good child. But that was absurd, because if they were taking care of anybody, it was Eric.

I stayed in the hospital ten days. When we went home to Mrs. Tompkins', it was spring in Washington, and along every curb were barrows of spring flowers—daffodils and hyacinths and white tulips.

Miss Hammond and Eric had the room next to mine on the fourth floor. Miss Hammond did what was called in those days eighteen-hour duty, which meant she slept there with the baby and went off for a few hours every afternoon. It was Mrs. Tompkins' delight, she said, to look after the baby while Miss Hammond was out. Those afternoons. I would take a long nap, and then we would go out and push the baby in his father's old perambulator along the flower-lined streets, to join the other rosy babies in Dupont Circle, where the little children ran about in their matching coats and hats of wool— pink, lavender, yellow, and pale green.

It was an orderly, bountiful life. Breakfast was at eight, and Mrs. Tompkins dispensed the coffee from the silver *repoussé* service before her, and herself broke the eggs into their cups to be handed by the butler to Miss Hammond and me. We had little pancakes with crisp edges, and the cook sent up rich, thick hot chocolate for me to drink, because I had not yet learned to like coffee. In those days, a thing like that did nothing to my figure. When we had gone upstairs, I would stand in front of the mahogany mirror in my bedroom, sidewise, looking at my new, thin shape, flat as a board again, and then I would go in to watch Miss Hammond perform the daily ceremony of the baby's bath—an elaborate ritual involving a rubber tub, toothpicks with a cotton swab on the end of them, oil, powder, and specially soft towels—and the whole room was filled with the smell of baby. Then it would be time for me to nurse Eric.

I used to hold him in my arm, lying on my bed, and it was as though he and I were alone inside a transparent bubble, an iridescent film that shut everything else in the world out. We were a whole, curled together within the tough and fragile skin of that round bubble, while outside, unnoticed, time passed, plans proceeded, and the days went by in comfortable procession. Inside the bubble, there was no time.

Luncheon was at one-thirty, Amos and Andy was at seven, dinner was at seven-thirty, bedtime was at ten-thirty, in that house. The servants made excuses to come up to the fourth floor and look at the baby, and lent unnecessary helping hands when the butler lifted the perambulator down the steps to the street for our afternoon walk among the flowers. The young mothers I had met came to see the baby, and Mrs. Tompkins ordered tea with cinnamon toast served to us in the drawing room afterward; they talked of two-o'clock feedings, and the triangular versus square folding of diapers, and of formulas, and asked me to lunch at the Mayflower, early, so that I could get home for the early-afternoon feeding. But the young mothers were still strangers to me—older women. I did not feel anything in common with their busy domestic efficiency.

The spring days passed, and plans matured relentlessly, and soon it was time for me to go home to New York with the baby, to the new apartment Tom had taken and the new nurse he had engaged that Mrs. Tompkins was going to pay for. That was simply the way it was, and it never occurred to me that I could change the plans. I wonder what would have happened if a Dr. Lawford had marched in and given me an order. . . . But after all, I did have to go back; New York was where I lived; so it's not that I mean. I really don't understand what I do mean. I couldn't have stayed at my mother-in-law's indefinitely.

I don't remember starting to wean Eric. I remember an afternoon when I had missed several feedings, and the physical ache was hard, and Mrs. Tompkins brought the baby in for me to play with.

I held him in my arms, that other occupant of the fractured bubble, and suddenly I knew that he and I were divided, never to be together again, and I began to cry.

Mrs. Tompkins came and took the baby away from me, but I could not stop crying, and I have never again cried so hard. It never occurred to me that anything could be done about it, but we were separated, and it was cruel, and I cried for something. I wish I could remember exactly what it was I did cry for. It wasn't for my baby, because I still had my baby, and he's grown up now and works in the Fifth Avenue Bank.

After that, time changed again for me. It flowed backward, to the memory of the bubble and to the first high moment in the hospital when I was Joan of Arc. We left Washington on a morning with the sun shining and barrows of flowers blooming along the curb as we went out the front door and the servants lined up on the steps to say goodbye. Eric was in a pink coat and a pink cap to match, with lace edging. But he didn't really belong to me any more—not the old way. I remember Mrs. Tompkins had tears in her eyes when she kissed us goodbye in the Union Station. But I felt dry-eyed and unmoved, while time flowed backward to that night we drove to the hospital in the middle of the night and she put her ring on my finger.

Of course, when we got back, New York looked marvelous. But even while I was beginning to feel all its possibilities again, time still flowed backward for me. I remember when it was that it stopped flowing backward. I was in someone's room in the St. Regis, where a lot of people were having a drink before going on to dance. I sat on the bed. A young man I had never seen before sat beside me. He said, "Where have you been all my life?"

And I said, "I've been having a baby."

He looked at me with the shine gone out of his eyes, and I realized that there were no possibilities in a remark like mine. I laughed, and reached out my glass to whoever the host was, and said something else that made the young man laugh, too. And then time stopped flowing backward and began once more, and for always, to hurry forward again.

So that is what I wonder about, all these years later. What it is that makes time hurry forward so fast? And what it is that can make it stop, so that you can live in now, in here? Or even go backward? Because it has never stopped or gone backward for me again.

It isn't having a baby, because I've had four, God help me—two by Tom, counting Eric, and two by Harold, not to mention that miscarriage, and although I hoped it would, time never did anything different again, just hurried on, hurried on.

It isn't as it occurred to me once that it might be, getting free of men in your life as I was free of them long ago with Mrs. Tompkins. Here I am, rid of my husbands, and the younger children off to school now, in this apartment. It isn't big, but I have day beds in the bedrooms so that every room looks like a sitting room for when I have a party. I'm free, if you want to call it that, and my face isn't what it was, so that I'm not troubled with *that* kind of thing, and yet when you might think life would slow down, be still, time nevertheless hurries on, hurries on. What do I care about dinner with the Deans tonight? But I have to hurry, just the same. And I'm tired. Sometimes I imagine that if Mrs. Tompkins were still alive, or my father, even . . . But they're dead and nobody remembers them any more, nobody *I* see.

1954

Who Lived and Died Believing

—◆◆◆—

*I*t was a strange, hot summer. The days throbbed and the nights were exhausted and melancholy. In August the temperature rose over ninety and hung there; the heat shimmered over the buildings and the streets of the town. Every afternoon at two Elizabeth Percy came down the steps of the house that was made into apartments for nurses. She walked along the burning pavements, around the corner, past the newsstand where the magazines hung fluttering on lines of wire, to Massey's Drugstore.

Her hair was very dark and as smooth as dark brown satin; it was combed back from her calm forehead and fell curving under at the back behind her ears. She wore plain uniforms with small round collars close about her neck, and she was all white and fresh and slender and strong.

From the heat outside she would walk into the dim coolness of the drugstore that smelled of soda and candy. There was a faint sweat upon the marble of the soda fountain; Mr. Massey and the other clerks stood about in their light tan linen coats, and they smiled at her without speaking. Dave was behind the prescription counter wrapping up a small package; first the white paper and then slowly the thin bright red string. He lifted his head as she walked down the center of the store to where the tables were, and his eyes met Elizabeth's. She sat down at the small black table and one of the boys from the fountain came and took her order of Coca-Cola. Several electric fans whirred remotely, high on the ceiling. The door opened again at the front, and three interns from the hospital came in. They leaned together on the marble counter in their whites. Their faces were young and pale with heat.

Dave came around the corner of the counter, and sat down beside Elizabeth. Mr. Massey walked slowly up toward the front of the store; he smiled absently at them; he always smiled at them as they sat together between two and three.

They never talked much. Elizabeth sucked the drink slowly through a straw, and lifted the glass and let bits of crushed ice drop into her mouth; they melted on her tongue. She loved to look at Dave. He was very thin and tall and he had straight yellow hair that fell forward in a lock on his forehead. His eyes were restless. He would glance at her suddenly and smile.

"How you doing over there?"

"She's just the same."

"Long case."

"Unh-hunh. Going to be longer."

"Tough you have to nurse one of those cases. Beckwith have any idea how long it'll be?"

One afternoon Elizabeth said, "Grainger told me yesterday he said he was going to use shock. Maybe."

"Insulin?"

"No, I don't think so."

Dave raised his eyebrows and shook his head. The damp yellow lock trembled against his forehead. He had finished the second year of medical school and was working at Massey's during the summer months.

"Oh-oh. That won't be so good."

"Grainger'll have it, in the mornings."

"No, no fun," he said.

"I'm so sorry for Mrs. Myles."

Dave shrugged his shoulders.

"Don't get tough," she said. "You're not a doctor yet. Beckwith's sorry for her, too. It's not the usual thing. She's gone through plenty."

"Sure," he said.

"Oh, real doctors have pity, you know; it's just you little boys."

She smiled at him, and he smiled back after a minute. He looked restless and impatient. He reached one hand under the table and put it on her knee, and looked into her long, calm, dark blue eyes.

"Meet you at eleven?" he said. Elizabeth nodded. He took his hand away.

"She wants to see you again."

"Oh, God."

"It doesn't hurt you any. Just go up there to her room for a minute and say good night. She gets so much out of it."

He gave a sort of groan, and shifted in his chair.

"She's got those damned eyes. I don't mean anything. I don't like her looking like that."

"It's just because we're going together," Elizabeth said. "It's the only thing outside herself, you see, like the only thing that's outside and ahead, and she likes to think about our going together."

"Oh, God."

"She asks me about you every day. Lots of times. I don't know whether she forgets she's asked before or whether... Come on, do it again once. It doesn't hurt you."

"All right. All right. Eleven."

"Eleven."

She got up and walked to the counter and laid the check down with a nickel. She went out into the heat, crossed the street, and walked up the wide steps of the hospital entrance.

In Copperthwaite Two the corridor was dim and hot. Elizabeth stopped at the desk and turned over the leaves of the order book. Doctor Beckwith had ordered the shock treatment for the morning; no breakfast. Elizabeth drew in her breath. Miss Grainger came out of the door of 53 and down the hall, without her cap.

"Hi," Elizabeth said.

"Hi."

"See you've got it ordered for tomorrow."

"Yeah, man."

"Does she know about it?"

"I'm not sure. He came up and went over her this morning, heart and all, before we went out. Told her, but not exactly said they were going to give her a treatment and there'd be acute physical discomfort. I love Doctor Beckwith. Discomfort. I don't look forward to it, I tell you. Seems like there's some things you don't get used to, and I don't like shock."

"What have you all done?"

"About the same. Walked. This walking miles in this weather does me in. I'm going home and go to sleep."

Elizabeth flipped back the pages of the order book.

"What is this stuff, anyhow? We didn't have it, then."

"Oh... camphor derivative? ... something. Reckon I'll know plenty in the morning. How's Dave?"

"Fine." Elizabeth said. They parted and went along the long

corridor in opposite directions. Elizabeth pushed open the heavy door of 53.

Mrs. Myles sat beside the open window and in the vicious heat observed passing back and forth outside (along the pavement?) back and forth from hell the doughy and grimaced faces of the damned. And a little part of the rotted grapes that rolled about within her brain watched the faces with an abstracted care; each of the faces was forever familiar, a face seen before (where?), seen before and seen again, and where, where, had been the face before? In her brain the fruit gave out a stench that she could taste in her mouth, and with it came the horror; no, no, those faces she had never seen before; it only seemed that she had; and the seeming was wrong and she could not send it away, the seeming stayed, shaking its tattered locks and grinning; yes, these faces had been seen before. The faces passed, and none of them was his. Watch, watch, observe with shrinking but insistent care each hideous face that comes nearer and nearer with death in its eyes and the unbelievable humanity, the bigness, in the coming-nearer mouths, until each face passed and was not his, was never his.

Her heart that was no longer her friend beat frantically one two three four five six seven eight eighty is a normal pulse for a woman seventy for a man but this was—hundred and forty... MAD.

The heavy-strained tension split with the scream of silk. The door opened and Miss Percy came in. So cool so calm so bright. With calm brow, with dark hair, and eyes like dark blue water. Cool as the little leaves that tremble in the tree. What thou among the leaves hast never known . This she has never known, with her calm eyes. Oh reach to me, thou among the leaves, reach down to me in hell with your cool hands, reach down to me.

She sees it all clean. The same world, clean. It is just me. I must remember that, it is just me; the world is cool and calm and bright. Not this. It is just me. Not mad, he said, just an exaggeration of your understandable state of tension, just an exaggeration of a normal point of view, just an exaggeration but not mad.

"Poor old Mr. Duggan next door's making quite a lot of noise," Miss Percy said, smiling. She stood before the mirror of the yellow-oak bureau and took her cap from the bureau post and pinned it to the back of her dark head. "I hope it doesn't bother you too much. Anyway, we'll go right out."

"Poor Mr. Duggan," Mrs. Myles said. "Is he getting any better at all?"

"I think they're going to give him some treatments that will make him all well."

The nurse glanced quickly at the patient.

She didn't mean to say that. She doesn't know if I know it, too. They are coming.

"You'd better wear your wide hat," Miss Percy said. "The sun's real hot this afternoon."

Obediently she put the hat upon her head and tied the ribbons that held it on under her chin.

"Put a little lipstick on," the nurse said. "It's so becoming to you to have a little color in your lips. Don't you remember what Doctor Beckwith said when he met us outside the steps yesterday, how pretty you looked? You've put on a pound and a half in two weeks. It won't be long before we have you weighing what you ought to. Before you know it you're going to be right strong."

Now to smile. Now widen the corners of the mouth and look straight into Miss Percy's eyes and hold it for a moment. But no! This is no smile. This is the terrible and tragic shape of a comic mask. Thus grimace the damned, who burn in the fires, and looking upward to the cool hand that is stretched in kindness and impotence to meet their torment, try one last time and achieve the horrible stretch, the grin, of the comic mask.

They walked down the hot dim corridor and turned to the right.

"Can't we please go down in the elevator?" Mrs. Myles said. Miss Percy's face looked troubled.

"I know," she said. "Only he wants you to walk through the hospital."

"All right."

So once again. Endure, endure. Endure to the end.

First they walked through the children's ward. Once it had not been bad; the universal slime had not had time to foul this too; she had seen them as children, delicate and pale and sweet. But then the tide of the slime had mounted here too, and ever since it had been this way. Student nurses, nurses, interns passed them. "Afternoon, Mrs. Myles." They all know me. Can they see it in my face? ... In the little beds the children lay or sat, with their sick faces. Sickness was everywhere. This is the great house of sickness. The children's faces were greenish with the heat. Which among them is mine? He is dead. He is not dead; which among them is mine, not well and laughing, but sick, which among them is my sick, corrupted child, infected from me all its tiny beginnings with the worm of sick sick sick? I am sick and all of mine is sick.

And she smelled the sharp recurrent fear. Fear, that clawed at the ruin of her mind; fear that rattled in her chest about the flabby palpitating boundaries of her heart. This fear is wicked, she thought: I am not afraid *for* the children, I am afraid *of* them. I am afraid of everything. I am full of poison of wickedness and fear; cold poison.

"He wants you to face things," Miss Percy said as they passed through and beyond the men's ward. "You know. Not get so you think you couldn't do something, special."

"I know."

In the beds the men lay, with sickness floating in the pools of their eyes. They passed on through the women's ward. A woman looked up. One side of her face was swollen out to huge proportions, and covered with bandages through which leaked sticky, yellow stuff. There was the long ominous smell of sweet ether and they passed suddenly across the hall of the hospital and their feet sounded sharp and loud on the stone flagging, and they went out into the loud sad heat. They descended the steps and started to walk down the road away from the town.

Suddenly from behind in the sunshine blared a loudspeaker, carried on a truck painted silver, with huge letters advertising an air-cooled movie house downtown. Slowly, slowly, the truck crept along the hot street. The enormous screaming music shook the atmosphere:

Fall in love, fall in love, says my heart…
Fall in love, *FALL IN LOVE…*

It swung slowly around a corner, out of sight. From far away in the afternoon the idiot voice still screamed:
"Fall in love, fall in love, says my heart…"
They walked steadily on, the nurse with a secret little smile; the woman, with a stiff and empty face.

The hours passed in gross and threatening procession. And with the hours the woman felt the always coming on, the rising walls, of the enclosing fear, like sound-proof glass, shutting her away; the terrible pawlike hand fumbling with the cork to stopper her finally into the bottle of aloneness.

She sat beside the window in the decline of the afternoon, and her hand was too sick with fear to stretch out to the shade and pull it down against the sun. She did not dare to move her hand. And soon the sun had bobbled behind the dreadful mountains of the west.

The nurse spoke to her several times and at last in her closing bottle she heard the voice from far away and turned, and it was supper being put before her on a tray. In the bowls of all the spoons were faces, that grinned at her and twisted their mouths into screams.

She ate, and then she was sick and the good food left her body in protest and she sat again by the window where the evening light now ran in around the edges of the shade like liquid poison, wet and lying on the floor and on the furniture of the room. The nurse put a table before her and laid out cards for a game upon its surface.

She looked down and saw the ferret faces of the kings and queens, the knaves; pinched and animal-like faces that whispered until the whispering was like a whistling in the room; and she turned her face away, but there was only the faraway flapping shade with the night running in around the edges, and she looked again at her hands but they were vast and swollen and she turned away and closed her eyes but within her was nothing but fear.

"How do you feel?" the nurse said in the evening room.

"How do you feel?" the nurse said.

"How do you feel?" the nurse said.

"HOW DO YOU FEEL?" the nurse said.

The nurse said, "Mrs. Myles, is there anything the matter?"

"It's as if," she said, "All the human things had been taken out of me and it left holes, like a cheese with great empty holes. And the holes have to be filled with something and they are all filled up with fear. So that where I had all sorts of things now I haven't got anything but fear in all the holes."

But that wasn't it at all, not only that; there was the bottle, how to tell someone of the bottle, glass, and sound-proof, where the stopper was being pushed tight home with her inside; not like a moth, no, not so clean, not like the souls in bottles, *animula, vagula, blandula*. No, like a festering purple lump of tissue.

Hell is not heat or cold, it is banishment to the ultimate ego. And in a few hours I shall be stoppered forever, she thought. I will not be able to speak, I will not be able to hear. I will be mad.

She asked for a pencil and paper. She wrote, and her handwriting was not her own; it was strange and inchoate like the sawings of the line of a fever chart. She looked at it with desperation. Will I scream? Will I groan? Will I grimace and mouth meaningless words? What will I do, with all of them watching me, crawling loathsomely inside the bottle, the face plastered on the purple stinking tissue like the fearful little faces in the spoons; while they watch, with their cool, well eyes, dressed all in white.

She tried to explain about the bottle on the paper with her failing handwriting, and then she folded it and wrote the doctor's name outside.

"Put it somewhere," she said urgently. "I want you to give it to Doctor Beckwith tomorrow if… if I…"

If I can no longer communicate what I feel, if I am mad.

"You're going to be fine," the nurse said. "You're going to be fine. Nothing's going to happen to you. Don't be afraid."

She thinks I mean die. No. Only the bottle. Or die?

Or die? For they are coming in the morning with something in their hands. For they are coming in the morning, footsteps measured, slow, down the corridor to me, bearing… the cross? … in their arms. No. No., You can still endure a little, do not think of Christ, that's the beginning. When the stopper is jammed at last deep into the neck of the bottle, then it will all be thoughts of Christ. Just with the last resisting inch, I can avoid the thought of Christ….

But Christ. So cool, so calm, so bright. O Jesus thou art standing outside the fast-closed door. Jesus with his mild face, his mournful eyes, the bright brown beard, the suffering. Oh, no!

The minutes, the hours passed in ever-gathering procession. Miss Percy ran water and opened the high, narrow bed and helped the woman into it.

"Dave is coming to say good night to you" she said above the bed.

"Dave is coming to say GOOD NIGHT TO YOU," she said. Oh… Dave is coming to say good night to me…. Dave? I don't know what is that word: Dave. Something; once; better; but not now. Only the bones of ego smelling of fear and dirt.

"Mrs. Myles."

"Mrs. Myles."

"MRS. MYLES!"

She turned her head and in the doorway, unreal, remote, beyond hell, they stood, the nurse, white and slender, and the young man—he was Dave. They stood there, down a tiny vista beckoning, the last reminder. For they were love. It still endured, somewhere, upon the fading world. It was a flickering candle point upon the dark; flickering in the waves that even now, like the great winds of hell, blew the candle flame, tiny, tiny.

The woman on the bed strained toward what she saw. Upon these bones of ego hangs one last shred of flesh, and as long as it hesitates there, gnawed by the mouths of cockroaches, so long that shred of flesh shall reach, shall strain toward what it sees, toward love. The shred is hanging by a nerve, and the candle point flickers and grows far, far away at the end of the cone-shaped darkness.

"Good night, Mrs. Myles."

"Good night," she said. "Are you going out somewhere together?"

"Unh-hunh," Miss Percy said. "Reckon we'll go for a drive in the country to find a breeze."

"Yes," the woman said. "I hope it'll be cool, in the country. I hope you have a lovely time. I hope you're happy."

She turned her head away from the door and closed her eyes, struggling to maintain that point of light somewhere in the darkness that was growing. As long as I can see it the bones will not be wholly bare, and the world not gone. I hope they will be happy. They love each other. Here I lie: in my sepulcher, and the stopper hovers, and the smell of brimstone everywhere. But while the candle flickers I will remember. When it gutters and goes out, I will go out, and the shred of flesh shall drop at last and the paw that reeks shall push the stopper down....

"Well, if you need anything, you know you just have to ring and Miss Perley will get it for you, dear. Good night," the nurse said.

But that, the woman did not hear.

After eleven the hospital was quiet and the lights along the corridors were turned out, so that only the light over the desks of the nurses in charge shone. The wards were dark and still; along some corridor could be heard occasionally the rattling trundle of a stretcher being pushed in a hurry, the stifled coming and going of a night emergency.

Elizabeth Percy went out through the hospital to the main entrance with Dave. A yawning nurse behind a desk raised her eyes and said "Hi!"; a doctor came hurriedly along the passage, wriggling his arms into a hospital coat as he went; his head was down and as Elizabeth passed he glanced upward from under his brows, nodded, and said, "Miss Percy...." They came out onto the open stone flagging of the entrance hall where lights burned behind the admittance desk, and went down into the melting melancholy night.

Elizabeth put her hand through Dave's arm and squeezed it; he glanced down at her and smiled.

"How you, babe?" he said.

"A little whipped.... That case is so hard, you can't do anything for her much and she's going through something awful."

"Forget it," he said. "You're off now. Climb in. Reckon it'll hold together a little longer."

She got into the old Chevrolet parked by the curb in the darkness.

They drove through the subsiding lights of the town, past the movie theatres with their electric signs turned off, now; the few people in light clothes dawdling before the doors of ice-cream parlors; there was the faint occasional hoot of a motor horn, the slam of a front door. As they passed into the outskirts of the town, the smell of the honeysuckle met them, drifting in from the country, and from far away the small sweet sawing of the crickets in the fields. They crossed a bridge and drove out along the country road, like a tunnel of darkness covered over with the branches of the trees. Their headlights made a white passage down the center of the tunnel. The smell of honeysuckle grew stronger, filling the whole night air, and sometimes they would pass a spot where the honeysuckle smell grew suddenly sharper, sweeter, bursting like fresh fountains into scent.

"My, this is nice," Elizabeth said. Her head was leaned back against the back of the seat.

He pressed her knee with his right hand and drew it toward his.

"Heat like we've been having can't last much longer," he said. "Registered over a hundred outside the store this afternoon. Got to crack sometime. May Leeds says her father and all the farmers are praying for rain."

"How's May?" Elizabeth asked in her low, quiet voice.

"Oh… I just took her to a movie while I was waiting around for you. She just dropped in while I was finishing up…. I've got to do something with the evenings, haven't I?"

"Of course, darling."

"It was a lousy movie."

She said nothing.

Far out along the road Dave stopped the car off to one side, under the boughs of the trees, and switched out the lights so that nothing could be seen; only the wide dark; the smell of the honeysuckle quivered through the darkness, and in the field beside them a whippoorwill called. Dave lit a cigarette and put his arm around Elizabeth.

"God, it's good to get out of that hellhole," he said.

After a moment Elizabeth spoke.

"I can't get Mrs. Myles out of my head," she said. "She just doesn't get any relief at all."

"Oh, skip the hospital when you're out of it."

"I know. Only I keep thinking that's what love can do to you."

"Inability to adjust."

"Yes, I know. But I guess it isn't so easy to adjust when you're too much in love, and then everything sort of came on her. I can't help picking things up. She was just mad about him and apparently he never cared much about her and she knew it, and that must be just … awful. And then when she got pregnant he went off with this other woman, and when she had her baby it died right away. Placenta previa. It would take quite a lot of adjusting.

"Well… Skip it. You can't go stewing about patients' problems. Leave that to Beckwith. How about kissing me?"

"You'd think she'd be through with love, wouldn't you? But she sort of hangs on to the idea of it. Like about… us."

"Yeah. Listen, I'm sorry, but I can't go up there any more and represent something for your patient. It just makes me feel too God-damn gummy."

"You don't have to. You never had to, only she seemed to get so much out of seeing you and it's awful seeing her every day, so lost. Anyway, she's getting shock in the morning."

"She is?"

"Yes. I hope it'll do the trick."

"How about skipping the hospital, baby? You're supposed to be a nurse, not an angel of mercy. Quit brooding about work out of hours. Kiss me."

She put both arms around him and kissed his mouth. His arms came around her and she felt the restlessness, the impatience in his body, and the eagerness, the searching.

"Oh, darling," she said. "I guess I'm pretty much in love with you."

"I don't mind you one bit myself," he murmured.

She started to speak, checked herself, and then spoke. "Dave, darling, you wouldn't hurt me, would you"

"Mmh-mmh."

"You could hurt me so easily. I'm so wide open to you."

"That's just the way I like you," he said, and he put his mouth down on hers, and his hands passed down her arms. Now they were close together, closer and closer in the satin darkness, and in the field the bird called at intervals and the smell of the honeysuckle came down in waves of shuddering sweetness. Over the country where they were the night sky seemed to brood, hanging soft and thick and vast over the land. Far away a train passed in the darkness and across the fields Elizabeth heard its whistle cry three times, three times—ah, ah, aaaah.

When they drove back into town it was very late and the air had a false coolness; there was a little breeze that would go away with the dawn. Elizabeth leaned silent against the seatback. Dave sat up straight and drove, and talked about the coming year of work.

"We get Parsons in surgery and will that be something. You remember Jim Jencks from down Eliza County, he was a real nice guy, I used to see a whole lot of him; he just had one run-in with Parsons after another, and that's one reason, I guess, he isn't going to be able to come back this year. Hope I don't get fixed up wrong with the old bastard."

"What's Jim Jencks doing now?" Elizabeth said.

"He just went on home. The damn fool, he got married. That finished him. Reckon he'll be raising pigs the rest of his life."

"I didn't know he got married."

"Yeah. Lehman, Lemmon...? Married a nurse, anyway. Never had good sense."

Elizabeth made a small noise with her lips.

"Oh!... Beg your pardon! Only *you* know, the business of guys marrying nurses, the way they do.... You know just as well as I do."

"Yes."

He left her in the dark and empty street before the apartment house where she lived. In the silence of the town the car sounded noisily as he drove away. Elizabeth looked after the car for a moment and then she walked slowly up the brick steps to the house full of nurses asleep.

The woman in Room 53 was awake, passing from unconscious to conscious horror, as soon as the phlegm-gray dawn had filled the corners of the room. There was the relentless metronome beat of doom rapping everywhere. It could not be slowed, nor stopped, nor avoided, but beat faster minute by minute until at last the beat would fuse, would be, the footsteps coming down the corridor outside, bearing the thing that would be borne. The woman turned her head in an old and useless reflex against horror and stared out of the window into the gray light.

On the bank opposite the hospital window there were a number of little things, moving about and pecking, and she knew that they were birds; but they were not birds, they were frightful lumps of mud, mud-birds, that jerked about the dirt. She turned her eyes away from them in loathing, but there was nowhere else to look. She closed her eyes upon the horror of outside, to meet the inside horror.

The chorus sang the evil hymns. O Jesus, thou art standing outside the fast-closed door. O Jesus, thou... the bright brown beard, the promise that is stained and filthied with corruption, and where is there to fly to lose this wickedness? Abide with me; fast falls the eventide. The awful sweetish dripping of the notes in chorus; that seems to be a promise, that asks for comfort.

The panic grew and the metronome beat, a little faster; the tentacles within reached out in frenzy and there was nothing there to grasp, only abide with me; fast falls the eventide; the dime valley of sin, echoing in the shadows. Though I walk through the valley of the shadow of death, I shall fear no evil; for thou are with me; thy rod and thy staff.... Were those what they would bear? The rod and the staff? Though I walk through the valley of the shadow of death.... I shall fear this evil, spreading like phlegm along the valley, everywhere, and all is evil, abiding with me....

Oh no! she cried inside herself with one last straining, no! But where was there to look? And in the ultimate necessity there flickered far off the pale point of the candle flame.

And then the footsteps down the corridor. And then the foossteps, am I dreaming them? The door opened and the priests and the acolytes came in—no, the doctor and the resident and the interns and the nurse—no the white-robed priests of this obscene observance, this sacrifice, and I am the sacrifice that lies quite still upon the altar, and they bear the weapon in their hands: the huge, brutal, long syringe lying upon a bed of gauze, and I am Christ to meet their sacrifice, to give my life. Six people in the room, and the sacrifice.

"Good morning, gentlemen," the woman said.

The nurse, by the head of the bed, laid her hand upon the patient's hand. The three interns stood grouped at the foot of the bed. The doctor stood on the right of the bed and looked down into the patient's face. The resident stood halfway down the left side of the bed, and in his hands he held the syringe.

She looked up into the doctor's face and upon it lay his eyes, flat, like gray, wet, cold oysters laid upon a plate.

"Listen," the woman said hurriedly. "Tell me quick. Does it matter what thoughts I am thinking? I mean will this fasten them permanently this way? Because my thoughts are so bad, and I can't seem to think any good thoughts...."

"It doesn't matter, kiddy," said the doctor. The eyes like oysters swam at her, and spun a little round and round. He laid his fingers on her wrist. The resident took her left arm and felt with his fingers along the veins on the inside of her elbow. She closed her eyes. Now let me think one good thought, that my brain may be embalmed in this sacrifice with a good thought held in it like a fly in amber. Oh, stay with me, flame, the point before the eyes, the one last point....

A wave from the outside of sick; of liquid; of shuddering horror ran up her veins.

"Thrombosed," the resident said. "We'll have to try another."

"Steady, kiddy," the doctor said.

Oh, flame, abide with me in the moment of dissolution....

Then crashingly a thousand carmine circles spun in her brain and there were crashed and mad carmine and the dark.

"Look at that," the leftmost intern said as the figure on the bed sat straight up, clenched in convulsion.

"Patient down on G Ward fractured three vertebrae in one of those," the resident said, watching.

"You'll have your good days and your bad days." The nurse's voice came to her. "You'll have your good days and your bad days, Mrs. Myles."

She was eating lunch off a tray and it was lettuce that she was putting in her mouth. It was thin and crisp and very cold. The world around her was hot and the sun beat through the window beside her. Everything was fatigue, and pain in her back, but the lettuce on her tongue was cool, and the nurse's voice; her name was Miss Percy and she was always there, in the revolving mist, speaking to her out of the wilderness, cool and clear.

"You'll have your good days and your bad days, Mrs. Myles."

She was walking through the jungle of the world, and she was lost. She did not know where she was. It was an utterly strange, green jungle. Only the nurse, Miss Percy, was there beside her, and so she continued to walk through this land.

They came to a brook that ran through a shady hollow and they sat down on a large stone by the margin of the brook and the nurse took off the woman's shoes, and she put her tired feet in the brook. The water was warm and fresh and ran softly past her feet. Beside the brook stood tall green trees that she had never seen before. She kept her feet in the soft running water and listened to the rustling in the leaves of the strange trees.

"How did I get here?" she asked. "Where have I been?"

The nurse's voice came with the sound of the brook, cool and clear.

"You're taking a walk in the country. You're staying at the hospital for a while."

"I don't remember. . . ."

"You'll have amnesia for a little bit. It's all right."

It's all right. . . .

Miss Percy stopped the doctor in the corridor.

"Doctor Beckwith, may I speak to you for a minute?"

The doctor stopped on one foot in his hurrying walk. The two horns of the stethoscope stuck up from the pocket of his white coat.

"My patient is getting hardly any sleep, doctor. I wondered if you could order something."

"Can't give sedatives, you know, with the treatments. Has a counteractive effect."

"She just seems so terribly tired."

"Well, she didn't even feel tired before…. I'll order insulin tonight, Miss Percy. See whether that'll put her to sleep."

"Thank you, doctor."

"You don't look as if you'd got much sleep yourself," the doctor said.

"Oh… it's just this heat."

"Got to break soon."

"Yes."

They were in a bowling alley, that was what it was, although she did not know where the bowling alley was or how she had got there. But the nurse was sitting on one of the wooden theatre seats behind her. She herself was standing, facing the alley with a bowl in her hand.

She continued with the action that somehow she had begun. She neither felt the bowl with her hand nor felt the floor under her feet when she moved forward. It was like moving through air. She willed herself to make the gestures that somewhere inside she knew should be made now, and her body carried out the commands, but without sensation, without seeming to touch anything at all.

It just shows what you can do, even though I am moving in air.

She let go the bowl and watched down the long straight alley where the bowl rolled, and heard the rumble of the falling pins.

She watched as the three black bowls came rolling up the wooden trolley to the side, and came to a stop. She picked up one of them and although she had picked it up she felt nothing against her palm.

It's almost fun, she thought, seeing what you can do by will power.

It was night, and suddenly she could not bear to lie in bed any longer. Since the nurse had stuck the needle in her arm the strangest energy and slow hope had begun in her.

In the dim spaces of this room the nurse was moving about. She was taking off her cap.

"I want to get up," the woman said. "Can I get up? I want to talk."

The nurse turned and smiled.

"All right," she said. She pulled forward the big chair that was by the window, and helped the woman into it. The nurse sat down on a small straight chair and smiled at the woman.

"But were you going away. . ." the woman said, puzzled. Something stirred in her head, faintly remembered.

"No," the nurse said. "I haven't anywhere special to go. I'd be glad to stay a little later, Mrs. Myles."

"You don't know," she said, "what hope can feel like. It's like running water. I mean freedom. Oh, you don't know what it's like! To be able to see freedom. Even just a little bit."

"You're going to have all the freedom in the world."

"I keep thinking of the loveliest things—long straight roads and driving along them fast in an open car. You don't know what hope can feel like. It's like the wind beginning to blow. Am I really going to be free?"

Suddenly the words of something whose origin she could not remember came into her head and she began to repeat them aloud: "That this nation, under God, shall have a new birth in freedom, and that government of the people, by the people, for the people, shall not perish from the earth."

Shall not perish..

"That's what I mean," she said. "That's the way it feels. I can't remember but it wasn't that way before, it wasn't by the people, for the people, I mean as if I were the people, as if I were a nation. A woman like a nation."

"Yes," the nurse said. "I know. Instead of under a dictator, you mean. It's awful to live under a dictator and not belong to yourself any more, isn't it?"

"Yes," she said impatiently, pushing that part away from her, for now there was hope, forming like a five-petaled flower, like a star. Sitting forward on the edge of the chair in her excitement, she repeated the words again, whatever they were: "This nation, under God, shall have a new birth in freedom—and that government of the people. . ."

And after some time the nurse went away and came back with a tall glass that was filled with sugared water, flavored deliciously with lemon, and the woman drank it.

And on some mornings the doctor and the resident and three interns came into her room, and the resident carried the large syringe. He was always the one who inserted the needle into her vein. It was a thing that came suddenly on some mornings and it had to be faced, once more; endure, she thought, endure to the end. And always at the last she summoned to her vision, with her eyes closed, of the candle flame, that companioned her through the darkness, through the bad days, through it all. It did not leave her, it remained to fortify her in the last extremity, when they came and the needle went into her arm and in her head spun the carmine circles and the world crashed, and then the dark. . . .

"Don't think she'll have to have another," the doctor said, as they watched the figure in convulsion on the bed. "This stuff certainly is magic in some cases."

On an afternoon in the yellow sunshine, suddenly she was sitting under an apple tree in the yard beside the hospital, and the nurse, Miss Percy, was sitting on the grass beside her. Mrs. Myles turned her head slowly and smiled. The heat had gone; it was a cool and lovely afternoon; the leaves rustled in the tree above her and from its branches came the smell of apples.

On the grass farther away some interns were playing baseball. Their voices shouted to one another, and the ball could be heard smacking their cupped palms. A breeze trickled along the air. The shadows were beginning to lengthen from the wall of the hospital, and in that light the interns, in their white clothes, ran and shouted. From a grass bank on the other side of the road from the hospital a bird called, suddenly, sweetly.

"Hello," Mrs. Myles said.

"Hello, dear. You're feeling much better, aren't you?"

"Yes," she said. Things were swimming back into her memory, the buildings here were taking their places in the world. And everything was very calm, very peaceful; there was no hurry. It doesn't matter.

She looked at the nurse, who had been there all the time. In the darkness and the long confusion, in that strange land where she had been, the nurse had been with her all the time. She studied the dark, smooth hair, the oval face, and the long, dark blue, quiet eyes.

"How is Dave?" Mrs. Myles said.

"You're remembering, aren't you?" the nurse said, without looking at the patient. "I think he's fine. I haven't seen him for a while."

"But…"

That did not fit. She stayed silent for a little time, while the remembrances slowly rearranged themselves within her head.

"But, you're in love with him," she said slowly. "It was you both. You are in love with each other."

"Well… You see, we aren't going together any more."

Something was wrong. Wait while the sifting memory slowly settled. Her own life was dead, somehow she had learned that, someone had taught her that in the strange, twilight land. She knew that she had been reborn and that this was a new life. She could never have the things of her own old life, for they had gone and they were dead. But one thing only... a candle burning down a vista, some constant star that had companioned her through the dark valleys of the land she had left.... She remembered two figures standing in a doorway.

"You're not?"

"No," the nurse said. She looked tired. They stared at each other and then a new and curious thing happened, a wave swept upward and from her eyes the woman felt tears falling. It was not despair. It was only deepest sadness. The last thing had gone out of the old life. Now the past was wiped black and she was all alone and beginning a new life, reborn alone. The purest, quietest sadness swept her and she could not halt the tears that fell and fell.

"You musn't mind at all, dear," the nurse said. But their eyes kept meeting the nurse's quiet and dry, the woman's full of tears.

The baseball game had broken up and a young intern came strolling by the apple tree, and looked down at the two who sat upon the grass. His face Mrs. Myles knew. It had looked at her on many mornings.

"Afternoon, Mrs. Myles, Miss Percy," the intern said, and then stopped in embarrassment at the tears on the woman's face.

"Well..." he said. "Seems fine to have a good cry, doesn't it?"

"Yes," she said, crying quietly, for all that was dead, now, forever, and could never be brought back. And it was fading fast. Fade far away, dissolve, and quite forget what thou among the leaves hast never known. It was all over; it was finished; the fight with death and sin, the wandering in the strange lost land. It was all gone, and love was gone too, and the candle flame had silently gone out. Above their heads where they sat upon the grass the little leaves in the apple tree whispered. It was all gone, and from now on the world was new, a page unwritten.

1942

Club Car

It was not an extra-fare train. It was not even one of those quiet, self-respecting trains that make their New York-to-Boston trip in a consistent five-and-a-half hours. It was just an unassuming old train that didn't pretend to take less than six hours, and really took seven; but it was the only one I could get a seat on, the day before Christmas, it never having occurred to me that anyone but myself would want to go to Boston on that day.

It wasn't a train to be proud of travelling on; it was even a little *déclassé*, with its stained-glass over-windows and varnished mahogany trims to the green plush chairs. Just a sound family train, full of middle-aged matrons, wearing toques made of artificial violets, and children going down the aisle to the water-cooler. Apparently, I was the only woman on it under forty. It racketed along, stopping at the most improbable stations, like Bridgeport and South Norwalk. This slovenly dallying awakened almost an affection in me; it reminded me so of walks along Park Avenue with my fox terrier.

But on the whole it was pretty dreadful. The poor old thing lurched so, and the lights flickered and the dining car wasn't opened until New London and everyone rushed for it at once, putting my mild thoughts of tea out of the running. The Pullman was exceedingly cold. It had been exceedingly hot, but now they had decided that it was to be exceedingly cold, and I had to sit in the rear corner, where great gusts of nice fresh New England air assailed me at each of the train's so-sociable stops. I thought I might be able to get my mind off that by writing some letters, but when I asked the porter for a table he brought me a time table. That sort of discouraged me, and I decided to make for the club car and befuddle my petulance with a cigarette. It seemed a long way off, there were a lot of cars named Myrtle and Hopedale, and I had to struggle through the crowded corridors, jammed with drummers who had witty remarks at their tongues' ends.

It seemed very nice in the club car. There was an absence of green plush and thirsty children. Through proximity I began to feel quite friendly toward the laboring old engine, plugging along through the dark, doing its best. It was good to have a drag off a Chesterfield.

But soon I became aware of suspicious eyes peering at me through the smoky murk. Elderly bank clerks, haberdashery salesmen, and students at Rutgers were eyeing me with distaste and antagonism. I became aware that I was not wanted. I became aware that I was doing something that wasn't done. I became aware that, thoroughly depraved through contact with dissolute extra-fare trains, I had violated a sanctuary. I had come into the club car, and I was a woman.

And they thought, beyond question of a doubt, that I was bent on seduction. The men nearest me carefully turned their backs on this creature of so light virtue and sedulously perused their newspapers. Those timidly curious creatures who caught my scheming eye blushed and stared fixedly out into a night they could not see through the thickly fogged windows. I felt desperately sinister without wanting to at all, an adventuress in spite of myself.

Far be it from me to destroy the decency of a man's refuge. There were two sections at the end of the car, facing seats that had a comparative privacy. I went and sat in one of these. I had no wish to bring sex into these men's sheltered lives, but on the other hand I was damned if I wouldn't smoke the cigarette I had struggled all this way for.

There was a man in the section opposite mine, an elderly man, with a yellowed mustache, smoking a corncob pipe in good, solitary, masculine gloom. I watched him. He ignored me and drew long draughts on his pleasant pipe, his eyes exploring the future, or, perhaps, the past. He seemed a nice, dreamy old man, a fit companion for my solitary smoke, one who had grown beyond vain thoughts of predatory women. Live and let live. He could smoke his pipe, I my cigarette. We smoked in silence.

His fading eyes now stared unseeing out into the night through the veil of a foggy window. His gnarled old finger wrote words, idly, on the steamy glass. What would a worn oldster like this have to put down, fleeting thoughts on a slate that the warmth of the next station would erase? Footsteps, thought I, sentimentally, on the soon-to-be-washed sands of time. I looked. He had written, shakily, "I am married."

Poor old thing. Posting his only defense against a bold adventuress. I went back to my wind-swept seat in my cold car.

1931

Essays on Hale's Short Fiction

The Laughter Downstairs:
on "The Earliest Dreams"

Ann Beattie

⸺ ⁂ ⸺

Nancy Hale was married to the eminent critic and classics editor Fredson Bowers and living in Albemarle County when I went to the University of Virginia to begin my first job after graduate school (a one-year position). I was twenty-seven. I wore funny T-shirts and often took my dog to class with me. Early on, I met Staige Blackford, the new editor of the *Virginia Quarterly Review*. He saw to it that I was introduced to Nancy and Fredson. Nancy liked me immediately when I wrongly assumed the flashy sports car in the driveway was hers, the more generic car his. I doubt that I wore a T-shirt and jeans to the Bowers', but I wouldn't swear to that. Nancy wore a silk dress. Fredson tapped out a bit of snuff, which he inhaled from the dimple between thumb and first finger. The most amazing moment—not at all funny when it happened— was when my then husband heard wrong, and mistook Fredson's mention of Bernard De Voto as a remark about the car, the DeSoto. Some hilarity ensued. Nancy and I realized why they were talking at cross-purposes before they did. How extremely kind she was: I was the new young thing at *The New Yorker*, where I had published a half dozen short stories within the past year, and would go on to publish more than forty others. But I may never catch Nancy, who had published upwards of seventy in *The New Yorker* by that time. And would have published more if they'd been willing. But there was little talk of that. Writers don't talk about their own writing. Also, extra manners were required because it was the South. Tea with lemon, or cream?

There are as many stories about childhood as there are autumn leaves. Sometimes the dryness results in unexceptional colors; other times the rain turns the leaves brilliant. Either way, as Barbra Streisand sings, it's always autumn. Metaphorically, of course.

Nancy Hale used metaphor as well as any other talented writer. And long before the now-popular, much-overimitated use of second person in Jay McInerney's *Bright Lights, Big City* and Lorrie Moore's *Self-Help*, she used the direct address in "The Earliest Dreams," the title story to her 1936 collection. The first sentence seems to set up the story as a fairy tale: "That was long, long ago." [1] The repetition lets the reader know that the writer knows that what will be told is a Story; also, that the writer doesn't want us to read this sentence neutrally and straightforwardly. If no echo—a literary wink of the eye—was needed, one "long" would have sufficed. So, in the first sentence, we readers are reassured (which in fiction almost always signals the opposite effect), and then "our" mind is read. The bed you or I slept in isn't the bed we begin to hear about, but we also know that we're expected to become the

---

[1] Hale 472

character: providing details reassures us. But since it isn't, of course, *our* childhood bed, there are two stories: our personal story (which, once conjured, acts as background), and the tale being told. The storyteller is convincing. Even polite enough—human enough—to admit to a bit of confusion ("What was it you wanted so?"[2]), whereas in real life, things proceed on the bizarre assumption that everyone knows, generally, what everyone else thinks, a notion that persists in spite of our lives filled with inevitable rude awakenings, strange revelations, unpredictable behavior. Still, the idea is sacrosanct: we know what our husband is thinking; he more or less knows our attitude toward Jon Stewart and whether Pommard is worth the expense. We know whether a friend prefers cats, dogs, both, or neither. (And just look at the times we've been confounded: the great dog lover buying a bird! And didn't you think Malcolm was *allergic* to cats?)

This takes me far from the world of this story, but expresses my notion of why readers are so often surprised, and why it's so easy to pull off. "The Earliest Dreams" is almost like a buzzing in the ear emitted by something that won't go away. Its adaptive strategies to avoid being slapped at are the seductive rhythms, the way the voice seemingly encompasses and envelops the character being spoken to, the facts that become "real" upon being recounted. The narrator's in charge because we *know* this narrator: it's the storyteller; it's Mama sitting on our bed. All nice-nice. (Be on guard against buying into that.)

> From miles and miles away you heard a late train breathing across the countryside, hurrying distantly through the white winter night to the yellow lights and the little quiet towns. Its whistle blew, so far far away, three times, Ah, Ah, Aaaah.[3]

---

[2] Ibid.
[3] Ibid.

Aaaah, indeed. Words repeated for emphasis, but also, I think, to point to the conventional method of telling a fairy tale, or even a story: a reminder of artifice. "Miles and miles" is a humming; "white winter"—its sounds are made by puffing out your lips; "little quiet towns" are a little tap dance of t sounds. Then your mouth puckers for the *w* of "whistle"— you're blowing again; not just the train, but *you* yourself. The author has thought carefully about the deliberately lovely phrasing of the story, about the way repetition can not only provide hyperbole, but also make you huff and puff, like the train. It's only fair: if the train can be personified ("breathing"), you, too, can be converted, imaginatively transforming into an object (the train). By the time we get to the whistle's "Ah, Ah, Aaaah," it seems clear we can read the words expelled two ways: as a sigh of relief, or as the last words uttered—the sound of death.

Death is the undercurrent of the story. In the first long paragraph, after the single-sentence paragraph that introduces the story, there seems to be so much understanding, so much empathy, yet the vagueness of "You longed for something" points to an almost Beckettian absence. (Or think of Joseph Heller's brilliant novel *Something Happened*.) *Something* can bring us up short, every time. The line concludes: "You longed for something, lying still between two smooth slices of sheet, but you could not think what it was, and now you will never know what it was."[4] The narrator reads the other person's mind, can't find the exact information (true, this might be because the other person can't), settles for the vague but ominous (or ominous because it is vague) "something," and gives us a series of words with the letter s that start us hissing. Notice also the contrast between the words "smooth slices"—a nicely cut bit of cheese is one thing; a "sliced" sheet is frightening.

[4] Ibid.

In the story, there are people downstairs, in the other world. It can't be known, especially to a child, exactly what they do or say. And since we, too, have been put in the place of a child, through the second person, then we, too, shiver when "all the laughter came upstairs suddenly in a gust."[5] When car lights illuminate the bedroom, they are frightening to us as well: "the lights scraped along the other wall."[6] Throughout the story, the uncomprehending child is aware of (or at least the narrator states that the child is aware—a distinction worth making) lights, sounds, and the images the sounds occasion: "the important clatter of plates" that are described as "fragile, impossible, fairy plates." They are expensive plates, they have socially ascribed importance, nevertheless they are "fragile" and might be in danger; they are "impossible"—I would assume impossible in terms of the child being served from them, eating from them carefully. As with the adults, the plates are to be both revered and feared; "fairy" reinforces the idea that began the story, of its being a kind of fairy tale, but the idea of "fairy plates" suggests that fairies are other, that there might be a magic realm inhabited by fairies, who eat from *their* special plates. The world of the imagination, holding open tantalizing prospects in one way, simultaneously excludes the child from participation.

All that laughter from downstairs, the mysterious laughter emanating from the adults, is also the Cosmic Laugh, the big joke on all of us. We're all in our little beds, vulnerable, uncomprehending. (And if we might not be in bed, that's usually where we return to die.) I think of the voice that addresses the child as a version of the information we've all internalized: a voice that— at different times in our lives—narrates a story we can't not hear. The voice is silent only at the end. At the end of the story. At the end of life. The story is not a parable, but it's an enticement—

---

[5] Ibid.
[6] Ibid.

a paradox of an enticement, really, since we might choose to avoid it if we could, but alas, we cannot. On the last page of the second section, we read: "You thought of the silent woods, where there were no lights and no sound, with perhaps the infinitely small track of an animal running momentarily under the trees in the dark." [7] "Momentarily" almost makes me jump out of my chair. And in case any doubt remains about what's really being narrated in the haunting capacitance of this story, we are told that "you alone were alive in this still, unbelievable world, in your own room with its long window." [8] Yes, we are all alone; yet we are the only ones who have our particular private moments.

The narrator conflates personal childhood memories with the memories of the person addressed. There is an adult's sense of what the distant music means, a sense of *schadenfreude* about its being conjured up: "You felt so sad, so happy and so sad, because something that was all the beauty and the tears in the world was over, because something lovely was lost and could only be remembered, and still you knew that for you the thing had not yet started." [9] Clearly this is projection—or, at the very least, not the terms in which the child would truly think. Perhaps the thing that "had not yet started" was adult life: a rather sad one, by this narrator's perceptions. Also, if we go along with the fiction that the child might really be listening to this narrative, what salutary effect would this pronouncement have? There's been a change, or a gradual revelation, and now the narrator is speaking to herself on the subject of sadness. Internal is conflated with external as "the quiet snow and the sky beat like a pulse." [10] The echo occurs in our own heads, our adult heads, where we've integrated the symbolism of the snow and the moon, where we understand that the seemingly ordinary yet evocative words are hugely charged.

---

[7] Hale 473
[8] Ibid.
[9] Hale 474
[10] Ibid.

The stunning last paragraph repeats what has by now become not only the sound track, but (I think) the status quo; the quintessentially ordinary laughter from downstairs transforms itself from being larger than life until it becomes demystified, inflated to symbolism, deflated to what we understand to be its understandable qualities. We nod in weary, grown-up acceptance of the metaphor the author has invoked, only to be undercut by the last sentence: "You never knew what things they laughed at when they laughed so long in the evenings, and now you never will know." [11] As one moves away from childhood, forgetting becomes a form of understanding—but why the flat pronouncement tinged with bitterness? It's more a taunt than a revelation; it sounds like the way one nasty child would speak to another, though a bit more eloquent.

The child addressed is the narrator's younger self, which explains the intimacy, the sporadically still-questioning mind, the necessity of remembering precisely, vividly, because in those sounds and images of the past, some clue might be found about the meaning of the present. If the "you" will never know, it's because life, like a story, moves on, and in spite of a narrator's capacity for stunningly acute description and viscerally remembered moments interspersed with poetic descriptions of the imagined world, finally beauty becomes secondary to the quotidian: the search for meaning comes to a cryptic end, as evenings devolve into night. Literary and metaphorical night. Finis.

Works Cited

Hale, Nancy. "The Earliest Dreams." *American Mercury* 31. April 1934. 472-474.

---

[11] Ibid.

ANN BEATTIE is the author of nine short fiction collections and seven novels, and has received numerous recognitions for her achievements in short fiction, including four O. Henry Awards, the PEN/Malamud Award, the Rea Award for the short story, an award from the American Academy and Institute of Arts and Letters, and inclusion in Updike's *The Best American Short Stories of the Century*. Beattie and her husband, Lincoln Perry, live in Key West, Florida, and Charlottesville, Virginia, where she is Edgar Allan Poe Professor of Literature and Creative Writing at the University of Virginia.

The Restropective Narrator:
on "The Empress's Ring"

Phong Nguyen

———∞∞∞———

Central to the short story "The Empress's Ring" is the question of whether the eponymous ring is in fact "too good for a child to wear," as the girl's nurse claims. For all the space within the story that Hale devotes to the feeling of loss surrounding the missing ring, the heart of anxiety beats underneath her want. Even as she digs around in the sand to find the ring, the nurse's statement troubles her, inviting the question, *Is she fit to wear the ring? Does she deserve it?*

The ring itself is "a little girl's ring that *was said to have* belonged to the Empress of Austria" [italics mine]. Revealingly, the narrator expresses a great sense of uncertainty as she claims its provenance: she "supposes" the empress in question "would have been" Elisabeth; she received the ring, "I think," on her eighth birthday; and she "was told" that a family friend bought the ring at auction in Vienna. More revealing still is the fact that the girl appears to conflate the empress who was said to own the ring and the family friend who gave her the ring ("I thought of her privately as a princess").[1]

---

[1] Hale 35

In the end, however, the ring's actual history matters little, as the narrator decides unequivocally that "it was the most beautiful ring, the most royal ring"—an observation that precedes the nurse's stern response, "Far too good for a child to wear." [2] What does it mean to say that the ring is too good for the child? That too close a familiarity with fine things will spoil her? Or that she was born unworthy of good things? And if the girl *believes* the nurse's claim that the ring is too good for her, will simply *waiting* to grow up suffice to make her worthy?

The nurse's glib statement, followed by her assertion that "You won't be wearing it to play," provokes the girl to wear the ring as an act of rebellion: "[N]obody—certainly not she—could understand the love I had for that ring, and the absolute impossibility of my ever losing something so precious." [3] When it turns out that the nurse was right—that the girl should not have worn the ring, as she *did* lose the empress's ring in the sand pile, as she had predicted—it strongly suggests to the girl the possibility that the nurse may be right about the other thing as well: that the ring was, in fact, "too good for her."

Regardless of whether it is, in fact, a ring that is better than its wearer, the neighbors do not seem to share the nurse's scruples, and they freely lavish expensive things on their daughter Mimi—most notably, equipping her playhouse with "real Dresden china" decorated with rosebuds. Those rosebuds in particular haunt the narrator with their beauty ("there was nothing, there could have been nothing, that would take the place of pink rosebuds"). That is, until the girl receives the empress's ring:

> It was a ring meant for a little girl to wear. It was real gold, and real turquoises. It was beautiful, and it had belonged to an empress.

---

[2] Ibid.

[3] Ibid.

It belonged to my hand. It was just the right size. In the morning sun, when I went out to play, its five turquoises shone in a curly row. Even all these years later, I can remember looking at it and feeling satisfied, complete, and happy. [4]

There is no justification, from the perspective of this adult narrator, for this feeling of complete satisfaction. Whether the ring actually belonged to an empress, or whether it was ordinary child's jewelry, she owned it so briefly, and so long ago, that her claim upon the actual ring is obsolete and irrelevant. Yet through the presence of the retrospective narrator, the ring has come to symbolize life's lost possibilities, the manifold selves that *might-have-been*. But more than representing the promise of a road not taken, the ring suggests a particular destiny that would have been categorically better: one in which the girl was unquestionably "good enough" to wear the empress's ring.

It is only after she lost the ring, after all, that the girl can assert confidently, "it had belonged to an empress," followed immediately by the equally definite statement, "It belonged to my hand." Having lost it, she now feels a greater desire for it than ever, and a stronger claim upon it even than when she wore it. Once believing herself to be deprived of beautiful things, with the gift of the ring the little girl came so near to owning something that possessed objective greatness—made of gold and precious stones, intricately made, owned by a royal—that she suddenly senses the vast distance between herself and the life of true privilege. The girl's first epiphany is that, in the melancholy words of Emily Dickinson, "Success is counted sweetest / By those who ne'er succeed." [5] And she sadly ascertains from this experience that she is not the possessor of beautiful things, but the appreciator of them from afar.

---

[4] Hale 36

[5] Dickinson 13

The retrospective narrator allows the author to develop two characters simultaneously: the adult narrator, and the child she once was. The advantage, for Hale, of using a retrospective narrator is that she is not limited to the immature voice of a child narrator, and the epiphanies are not limited to only that of which a child narrator would feasibly be capable. Hale uses the technique masterfully in "The Empress's Ring," without straying too far into the indifferent or the sentimental.

The mood of the present-day narrator is not nostalgia, exactly, but one of reluctant acknowledgment—of the influence of childish fascinations and childhood disappointments upon her present-day self. As the narrator establishes from the first lines of the story, "I worry about it still, even today, thirty-odd years later. I close my eyes to go to sleep at night, sometimes, and I am back at the old, disintegrated sand pile where I lost it, digging in the dirt-mixed sand with my fingernails to find my little ring." [6]

The bewilderment of the woman speaking these lines is palpable. How can she be so preoccupied by such childish concerns? But by the end of the story, we learn that this flashback to her digging through the sand pile refers not to her as a little girl, but to a somewhat more recent episode, albeit one still years removed from the present tense. Between the adult narrator and the-girl-who-briefly-possessed-the-empress's-ring is the adolescent, who was also haunted by the loss of the ring:

> [Y]ears later, in my teens, I would suddenly remember my ring, the one I had lost, and would go out to the sand pile, by now almost obliterated but still a definite area to me, and dig and dig. It had to be there. I never found it, but it was there just the same, somewhere in the mingled sand and dirt, within a definite space about ten feet square.

---

[6] Hale 35

Once, I dreamed that I had found it. It was when I was a young girl going to dances, and the dream was about the most irrelevant to my life that could be imagined. But when I woke, with the clear memory of finding the ring and seeing it lie in my palm with its banner of five little blue stones, my excitement and the verisimilitude were so great that I went out to the woodshed—in a beige crepe-de-Chine dress, I remember, that reached my knees; high heels, and my hair shingled—and began to dig once again. Then the telephone rang for me, or someone drove up in a car. But after the dream it was not finding it that seemed unbelievable.[7]

This second epiphany—that the ring is not temporarily missing, but lost for good, and that the better life is not waiting patiently at the end of childhood to confer worthiness, but the adult may instead hold on to her childish failings—is subtly different from the first. As an adolescent, she no longer *wants* the ring, per se, she *expects* it. And it was *not finding* the ring "that seemed unbelievable" to her.

Focusing so narrowly on the ring as a metaphor for the promise of a nobler, better life, we may miss the importance of the sand pile into which it is lost. The sand pile survives her adolescence, but is "disintegrated" and "almost obliterated." The real loss here may not be that the little girl fails to hold on to the empress's ring, but that in pursuit of the ring she destroys that sand pile into which she might have instead contentedly played.

The third and last epiphany in the story comes at the very end, when the retrospective narrator thrusts the reader into the present tense. The adult narrator has accepted the fact that the empress's ring is lost. She certainly no longer expects to find it, as she has long since moved away from the home where it resides. But the idea of another little girl discovering it, with no elaborate illusions concerning its origins, intrigues her.

---

[7] Ibid. 36-37

There may not be any sand at all; the place is sold, and the new owners may have fixed everything up, torn down the shed, perhaps even put up a new, properly fenced-in sand pile somewhere for their growing children. I don't know.

Perhaps if the old sand pile is still there, one of the new owner's children will one day really find my ring, for it is there somewhere. Perhaps the child— a little girl— will be poking about with a tin shovel and will turn up that scrap of gold with its five little blue stones. I wonder what she will make of it.[8]

We do not know the exact age of the adult narrator, but we do know that she is looking back upon childhood from a good distance. In the quote above, the narrator's final epiphany appears to be that, at a certain stage of life, if we are lucky, we cease to covet on behalf of ourselves, and invest in the happiness of others. Her conception of "one of the new owner's children" is strangely parental. If she herself will never possess the life of "good things" that she once strove for, that she used to believe she was owed, then perhaps her loss will be another little girl's gain. Furthermore, the other girl is free to construct her own narrative regarding the ring, and does not have to agonize over her own worthiness to wear it. In fact, the possessive now applies to her, and to her alone: it is now "the little girl's ring," and it is "the *empress's* ring" no longer.

Works Cited

Dickinson, Emily. "Success." *Poems by Emily Dickinson*. Mabel Loomis Todd, Thomas Wentworth Higgins, Eds. Boston: Little, Brown, and Company, 1922. 13.

Hale, Nancy. "The Empress's Ring." *The New Yorker*. 10 April 1954. 35-37.

---

[8] Ibid. 37

Mary the Un-Merry Widow:
on "Entrance Into Life"

Debra Brenegan

⸙

Hale grew up in a family of artists, readers, and writers. Her parents not only allowed Hale's sojourn into the creative arts, they expected it. In Hale's world, women's creative pursuits were deemed equal with men's and it was assumed that all Hales were born creative. Thus, Hale apparently escaped the trappings of subordinated self-esteem many women of her era were raised with and seemed to come from a genuinely supportive and egalitarian family. From a young age, Hale was encouraged to express herself and was taught to view the world as an artist does. Her work was supported and honed into excellence. Hale understood her privileged position during an era when not all children, especially female children, were validated for their talents and nurtured unequivocally. As Nancy Hale's granddaughter Norah Lind has noted, some of Hale's stories are autobiographically based, but the stories are not fixed memoirs; they are pliable enough to lend themselves to reader interpretation. Hale wrote from her experiences about what life ought to be like, but also from the perspective of what life is sometimes like when it takes wrong turns, as her own life seemingly did at times. Hale's attention to sensory detail allows her to paint images of scene and character readers have a hard time forgetting—images readers themselves recognize and identify with. Hale then uses these snapshot images to comment upon social issues—especially those concerning women—in a way that gets under readers' skin enough to allow for personal, and possibly, societal, contemplation and change.

"Entrance into Life" concerns a young, widowed mother, Mary, who takes her six-year-old chronically-ill son, Robert, to watch the graduation procession at an all-men's university. Hale's Hemingwayesque opening serves to ground the story's setting and plot:

> Young men hurried by with their gowns fluttering about their legs, carrying their tasseled caps under their arms . . . Robert kept close hold of his mother's hand as they joined the crowds and went and stood by a white column in the shade. As soon as they stopped walking and stood still, he began to cough again. After the coughing was all over he opened his eyes, and the sun was still shining and the people were wandering slowly across the grass and along the colonnade and he could hear the band. His hand that Mary, his mother, held was very thin and small. She squeezed it and looked down at him and smiled when he finished coughing. He looked so neat and small and clean in his white shirt and his little brown shorts. His hair was smoothed down with water. [1]

The air is full of excitement for the future of the young men, even as Hale depicts ill Robert, coughing, seeking shade, his thin, small self carefully nurtured by his smiling mother

---

[1] Hale 3

who keeps him neat and clean. Robert probably won't live to graduate himself. He stands, ironically, next to his healthy mother, who also won't graduate from this all-male school, even though she is now the head of the household and has a need for education and job opportunities equal to those of any man, including her dead husband. They watch the procession as the brass band plays "The Merry Widow." Mary tries hard to appear merry, but fails, especially when Robert repeatedly draws her attention to x-rays he has recently had looking for "spots" on his lungs. She continues her efforts throughout the next songs, "The Stars and Stripes Forever"—a nod to the "confusion of the war years," when Harry, presumably died, and "March of the Priests," code for the funeral processions of the war victims and for the almost priestly procession of gown-clad young graduates marching dogma-like to their fates "in whatever world" they'd inhabit as adults—certainly a world Mary cannot imagine as a woman.

As they watch the procession of young men, Mary tries to enter the day's celebratory mood, much as she did once before. Robert's father, Harry, had gone to the school, as had "all [of] Daddy's family," presumably, all of the men of the family, anyway. Mary, like the graduates' mothers, sisters and girlfriends, watches this graduation procession from the sidelines, as does her sick child, and she remembers watching Harry's procession years before. Hale writes of Mary's remembering,

> She had tears in her eyes. It was like a wedding, the ending to something. All the young men came marching past, who had grown up and done with schools, who had played football and listened to lectures and got drunk and now were going to start living, somehow, beyond the commitments and the regulations of children. In whatever world, they were grown up now.[2]

---

[2] Ibid. 5-6

NANCY HALE—107

Mary remembers Harry's graduation tearfully. She misses him, of course, but her tears also illustrate other regrets—that Robert likely won't graduate, and that neither will she. Both situations are sad for Mary to think about. She describes the pomp of the graduation as "a wedding, the ending to something." Just as graduation is the ending of boyhood and the beginning of a time males would "start living," Mary equates marriage as the ceremony when girls become women, wives, yet also as a time that is "the ending to something." The boys' pomp and the girls' pomp might seem equally joyful, but don't necessitate equally successful or satisfying futures.

Mary steers Robert toward home after the procession. Robert asks, "Will I go to this college?" Hale writes Mary's reaction:

> She looked down at his small, white face.
> When he was first born she had used to look in his scrap of a face to see a boy's face there and what it would be like. Now she was looking for a young man's face, a college boy's, one facing a grown-up world, of whatever kind. She shut her eyes because she could not find any such face; inside her eyes everything was dark gray and cold, and all at once it might have been the middle of winter. She did not know where to begin to look for spring.
> But when she opened her eyes the sun was still shining.
> "Yes, darling," she said. "All your Daddy's family went here."
> "Will you come and see me when I graduate?"
> "Of course I will," she said. "Of course I will."
> And from far away they could hear the brass band still playing bravely and triumphantly in the sunny afternoon.[3]

Mary is a good mother; she protects Robert from the truth of his uncertain future even as she cannot protect herself from the truth of her own uncertain future. As a young widow, she has lost her husband, will likely lose her son, and hasn't yet

___
[3] Ibid. 6-7

found her own way in life. She looks for the future Robert in his face and cannot see him, not only because she has a hard time understanding what men do when they grow up and face their worlds "of whatever kind," but because she herself is in this world, doesn't recognize it, and doesn't know how to navigate it. Everything is "dark gray and cold, and all at once it might have been the middle of winter." Mary is grieving and lost. She has come, instinctively, to the graduation procession to garner hope and joy from a circumstance that once provided it. But, the circumstances have changed. Harry's graduation was joyful because it signaled a grand beginning to his future, which, presumably, would be Mary's future as well. Harry's death inadvertently means Mary, too, dies, in some ways, even as she makes brave promises to Robert that she will cheer him on during his graduation procession (instead of preparing, perhaps, for her own such procession). The day is ironically sunny and the brass band plays bravely on as Mary and Robert head home, away from the real ceremony, away from any real participation in the world.

"Entrance into Life" shows characters that are doing anything but entering life—a dead young husband, his lost widow and ill child. Life has or is passing them all by and the characters' brave upper lips threaten to quiver with the knowledge. Hale's story introduces a great theme of the collection—the theme of women entering life and living it. This story illustrates how so many people watch the procession of life, don't really participate themselves, and attempt to extract joy from the accomplishments of others, instead of from the satisfaction of being fully immersed in life for oneself. Hale calls readers to join society, to look for their own springs—their fresh beginnings—and to throw off the shackles of conventional female roles in order to fulfill themselves, first, and then to help others find fulfillment, as well.

Works Cited

Hale, Nancy. "Entrance into Life." *The Pattern of Perfection.* Boston: Little, Brown, and Company, 1960. 1-7.

Debra Brenegan is the author of *Shame the Devil* (SUNY Press, 2011), an historical novel about the life of nineteenth-century American writer Fanny Fern. She teaches English and Women's Studies at Westminster College in Fulton, Missouri.

Images

Nancy Hale's father, Philip Leslie Hale, holding Nancy as a baby. Philip Leslie Hale supplemented his earnings as an artist by writing, teaching, and lecturing on art.

Sophia Smith Collection, Smith College

Nancy Hale with her mother Lilian Westcott Hale at their home in Dedham, Massachusetts, October 1915. Lilian Westcott Hale was a celebrated artist of the Boston school, and the subject of many of Nancy Hale's memoirs in *The Life in the Studio.*

Sophia Smith Collection, Smith College

Photo by Tony von Thelen / Courtesy, Mary Welby von Thelen

Nancy Hale was a frequent model for her parents. This charcoal drawing by her mother is unusual in position. Nancy agreed to sit for her parents with the requirement that she be allowed to read at the same time. As a result, her eyes are generally downcast.

Nancy Hale Hardin's face quickly became recognizable in New York's social columns, and she was selected by the *Torches of Freedom* advertising campaign to encourage women's smoking. Nancy Hale commented to her mother that her endorsement of the habit was an easy way to make money.

Torches of Freedom *Ad Campaign Publicity Photograph*

Nancy Hale's reputation and talent as a writer in the 1930s gained her access to New York's publishing giants, from Maxwell Perkins to Condé Nast.

Courtesy, Norah Hardin Lind

Photo by Toni Frissell / Courtesy, Norah Hardin Lind

Nancy Hale and her son Mark Hardin (1932)

Photo by unknown, digital photo by Tony von Thelen / Courtesy, Norah Hardin Lind

Family photograph of four generations (1930): from left to right, Nancy Hale Hardin, Lilian Westcott Hale, Mark Hardin, and Harriet Clarke Westcott. Harriet Clarke Westcott was a pianist who insisted that all her daughters refine a skill. Lilian chose art over music. Her own daughter, Nancy, studied art for two years before becoming a writer.

Photo by Dave Skinner / Special Collections, University of Virginia Library.

Nancy Hale, at typewriter (1969): During her early years in New York, Hale worked at *Vanity Fair* and *Vogue* and went out nearly every evening before writing late at night. When her publishing success allowed her to concentrate on writing, she worked for several hours each morning.

Betsy

The thing that must be established, she felt, was that she
was not like that at all. She had a ... of a
whereas she, the real she, was quite different. She had been
betrayed, indeed; but it was not the way he saw it. She
must make him see —

→ Betsy is indomitable; she keeps bobbing up; she makes
the world lovely intermittently and keeps returning to happiness
unless Marjorie she can't be licked. She moves steadily
toward future; a born mother —

→ Hector is guilt-ridden, necessarily to past always; the present
seems evil to him & the past is sometimes nostalgic,
always regretful

The pull between him & past vs future.

He: What do you want, anyway?
She: I want to be loved & to love —

Hector still impresses her terribly — she does not realize his inferiority
Of all the mingled agony and rage and suspicion and
shame and dreams and joy and exaltation of their life
together, now only the joy & exaltation seem to remain —
Synopsize N.Y., Christmas in Hampton — Lambert — up to
night of party.

She seems to have a clearer view of him; her
her view of him —

Then the big smash; again all he has suppressed;
his family, his a "Snobbery" his complacence,
all reduced in his contempt (out of inferiority)
and she must submit utterly to him
Illegitimate child — She agrees to anything

Sophia Smith Collection, Smith College

Nancy Hale's third novel, *The Prodigal Women*, became a blockbuster best-seller. This manuscript page shows Hale's rigorous planning during the pre-writing stage as she sketched out the personalities and motivations for each main character before laying out the massive novel's content chapter by chapter.

Above: Eudora Welty, Nancy Hale, and Mary Bass, 1970. Below: Gregorio Prestopino, Lael Wertenbaker, Nancy Hale, and Conrad Spohnholz in front of Savidge Library, 1975.

Nancy Hale was a frequent visitor to the MacDowell Colony, which inspired her as founder of the Virginia Center for the Creative Arts.

Essays on *The Prodigal Women*

Introduction to the New American Library Edition: on *The Prodigal Women*

Mary Lee Settle

A classic, Roger Shattuck has written, is "at the same time, a period piece and forever young." Nancy Hale's fascinating novel of its time, *The Prodigal Women*, first published in 1942, is such a work.

I interpret a "forever young" novel as one in which we find our timeless selves, our hopes, our fears, our neighbors, never-ending, never-changing sorrow and joy and pride. Anna Karenina is echoed whenever a woman has to choose between son and lover, Emma Bovary whenever a middle-class romantic makes a fool of herself; and all of us have known, identified with, and still recognize vestiges of the three principal women in *The Prodigal Women*.

To relegate a novel to history, or to condemn it as "dated," which is the pejorative way of saying the same thing, is to miss this very quality. But it is just as essential not to ignore a book's own view of its time. It is a view that can be found nowhere outside of good fiction, neither in the certainties of history nor in the lesser novels by contemporary writers who did not use their senses to record their surroundings.

The fact that *The Prodigal Women* takes place between 1922 and 1940 is irrelevant to its essential meaning. Yet it is, at the same time, a perceptively observed documentary of the mores of the period and the daily ways people lived.

It is too easy to categorize it as an early feminist novel. It most certainly is "feminist"—though the use of that word is far more "contemporary" than the book itself—but it follows the tradition that existed long before women began using a self-conscious language in their appraisal of where they were and what they wanted. Nancy Hale is, and it is not quite the same, the most essentially feminine writer I know. Her female revenges are as ancient as Medea or Electra. But neither does she condone the excesses of "feminine wiles." These, too, are punished—terribly.

The "feminist" novel, if that is what is meant by novels where men are interpreted in a less than heroic manner, goes back to the great classics by women. The list is formidable: George Eliot's *Middlemarch*, where Dorothea's choice between Casaubon and Will Ladislaw is hardly a choice, and which is enough to frighten any sensitive woman out of marrying; Ellen Glasgow's Jason Greylock in *Barren Ground*, the author's terrible revenge on Southern men for losing the Civil War and drinking too much; Edith Wharton's Newland Archer in *The Age of Innocence*, Willa Cather's Jim in *My Antonia*. Here they are—strong women, frail men—a genre, a tradition, and a revenge for all the natural insults that female flesh considers itself heir to. Like these great women novelists, Nancy Hale's women are more alive, stronger, both more sympathetic and more destructive than her men.

A contemporary critic compared *The Prodigal Women* to the work of Thomas Wolfe; I suppose because it was long. Nothing could be farther from the truth. Nancy Hale's prose is controlled, her sense of place precise and vivid. She had the gift of making places resonate behind her characters, and become a part of them. Her introduction to Leda March, one of the "prodigal women," is at the beginning of the book. Scott Fitzgerald wrote that a professional writer has "a sense of the future in every line," and within this lyric passage of an eleven-year-old girl walking in the woods, there is an ominous forecast of her destructive isolation.

> Now that she could be alone, she was happy ... The woods were old. Parts of them were virgin forest; none of them had been cut for a century. Stoney Road was a lost segment of an old post-road. The paths that led among the woods were the same trails that Indians had followed before the settlement of New England. She loved them. Through winters and summers she had learned to walk quietly like an Indian along the paths, setting her feet down without breaking a twig... It was as though in the woods her awkwardness left her and she became full of useful grace. She supposed that other people, in the real world, felt all the time as she felt here: knowing the land, sure of themselves and belonging there.

Leda March is the coldest and most self-concerned main character I can think of since Julien Sorel in Stendhal's *Le Rouge et Le Noir*. The second of the novel's three leading female characters, Maizie Jekyll, is a marvelous picture of what can happen to transplanted, and not very smart, twenties flappers, cheerleaders, or small-town girls (north or south), who try old female survival techniques in new environments. She has the self-destructive urge of the conservative, clinging to the old ways at any cost. In Maizie's case, inculcated "feminine wiles" are a way of life. She knows nothing else. They destroy her.

The third of the women is Betsy, Maizie's younger sister and Leda's first friend, used by her and then thrown away. Betsy is two women: The first is a bright, charming, lively young girl who works, plays, reflects the fashion world of New York in the late twenties and early thirties, falls in love lightly and out again, and accepts the world she finds herself in with more joy than anyone else in the book. In one magic moment she embodies all the longing of all those thirties girls to "go to New York City."

On an afternoon in June Betsy Jekyll Jayne stood on a curb on Park Avenue waiting for the lights to change... She was charming... she stood quite still, in a red print dress and jacket and a white straw hat with a red ribbon. She looked like a picture in a fashion magazine, all except for one heel which showed a hole above the shoe . . . She had never been afraid. She had never visualized defeat or despair or shame. She was like a shining, brown, uncracked nut.

The second avatar of Betsy comes after a sea change caused by what Hale must consider a disaster: falling deeply in love. In reaction to one of the nastiest men in modern fiction, Betsy develops into a closed-off, calm, strong earth mother who finally, in the most ancient woman's way of all, uses the man to make a mother of her, then tolerates him the rest of the time, instead of shooting him and dumping him down a well, as he richly deserves.

Betsy's world was round and compact and workaday; it seemed to her now that Hector roamed in some vast ringing stratosphere. He had left her world at a tangent... She cooked the summer meals, she bathed the baby, she swam and lay in the sun, she went to bed with Hector when it was night. His new preoccupation did not trouble her. She did not see how it affected her and her small full life... He had gone off and up in such a curve while she marched straight on from sunup to sun down.

Hector, first the lover, then the husband of Betsy, then the puritan sadist, reminds me of the definition by Dostoevsky of a minor artist: "He lived the life of a man of genius but he had no talent." Petty tyrant, demanding man, failed "artist," Hector is Hale's picture of the writer *manqué*. In one of the best scenes of the book, a Hollywood director who has gotten drunk tells him, and us (and we read it with true relief), the truth about Hector and his ilk.

The second of the men in the novel, James, cousin and then husband of Leda, begins as a very attractive young doctor, and seems to fade into a kind of dim civility. Maybe it is because he is Leda's victim. He ends up marrying her worst schoolgirl enemy, and it is hard not to wish them well.

The third, Lambert Rudd, is the most interesting and self-redeemed man in *The Prodigal Women*. He is, or starts out to be, a very good painter. But caught in the trap of the women, he diminishes throughout the book. First there is Maizie, who drives herself into recurring mental collapse and him into debilitating guilt by trying to change his home truths into promises. Then, at only one time in their lives do he and Leda have a chance to become what they seem meant to be—he a good painter, she a good writer.

But it is hard to see such a future for them. Buried in the character of Leda from the first scene is her classic fatal flaw: She has no heart. And buried in Lambert is his fatal flaw. He rides roughshod over anyone who stands in his way, and, alas, Maizie, square in the middle of his road, trying wiles she learned as a teenager in a Southern drug store drinking Cokes with her chums, is run over.

Her pathos is the only "dated" attitude in the book: such women were accepted in the thirties as tragic; now their self-destruction is recognized. She reminds me of a dreadful line in Noel Coward's thirties film, *The Scoundrel*, "I don't want your love handed to me on a platter like the head of John the Baptist or lying in the road where I can run over it...." The only two truly decent men are the two fathers, and they are both failures. One commits suicide, the other is seen mostly through the destructively critical eyes of Leda March.

What makes *The Prodigal Women* a joy and a discovery to reread is a quality that Nancy Hale's contemporaries in the forties could not have seen. They saw the women then as products of their environment; reading the book now we can see them in the added dimension of their times.

But it is all too tempting to see their attitudes toward men, their overdependence on their mates for fulfillment, and their acquiescence, as dated, until we read the morning paper. And there they are still, the battered, the victims of moral and physical sadism who had stood for it until the event—the shot, the beating—happens to make the headlines.

At the time it was first published, the honest sexuality of the book obscured both the structure and the characters, according to Nancy Hale. People tended to read it for its shock value. To a reader today that aspect of it seems very mild. Now, over forty years later, the sexuality can be taken for granted and admired for its honest picture of what life was, and is, like for women.

1988

MARY LEE SETTLE (1918-2005) was the author of the "Beulah Quintet," a series of novels that tell the dramatic history of West Virginia, including *Prisons, O Beulah Land, Know Nothing, The Scapegoat,* and *the Killing Ground.* She won the National Book Award in 1978 for her novel *Blood Tie,* and was co-founder of the annual PEN/Faulkner Award for Fiction.

Nancy Hale, The Prodigal Writer:
on *The Prodigal Women*

Trudy Lewis

––––⊶⊷⊶––––

New England Girlhoods

In her introduction to *A New England Girlhood*, Hale acknowledges a debt to *A New England Boyhood*, the autobiography of her grandfather Edward Everett Hale, who himself took his inspiration from an earlier *New England Girlhood* by the 19th century American poet Lucy Larcom. Larcom, perhaps the most famous of the Lowell Mill Girls, was the daughter of a sea captain and her rise from factory operative to published poet forms the prototypical arc of the mill girl experience. The mill girls are so fascinating in part because of their conflicted class status as organic intellectuals, in addition to the gendered nature of their labor and literary output. The Lowell operatives, largely products of middle class farm families, may have lacked formal education, but a significant number of them proved to be highly literate. After arriving in Lowell, they worked eleven to fourteen hour days in the mills. And yet, loosed from the bonds of the patriarchal family, their routine domestic needs met by the boarding houses, many of them found that they had extra energy to devote to their education. After hours, they read such literary works as the novels of Charles Dickens and Sir Walter Scott, the Romantic poetry of Shelley & Coleridge, the sentimental verse of Felicia Hemans, and the abolitionist ballads of John Greenleaf Whittier, a local with whom many were personally acquainted. They also attended lectures and formed "Improvement Circles" for the study of such subjects as botany, German, and literary composition, and began a literary magazine, *The Lowell Offering* (1840-1845), consisting entirely of the works of female factory operatives. This periodical, along with the associated Improvement Circle, became the matrix for several careers, most notably that of Larcom, who produced several volumes of poetry along with the reminiscence of girlhood, initially published in *The Atlantic Monthly*, where Edward Everett Hale would also publish his boyhood memoir.

Nancy Hale, the daughter of two painters, shared the literary enthusiasm, the middle class status, the ambition, work ethic, and conflicted class loyalties of many of these early factory girls. Although she was from a respected Boston Brahmin family, including literary luminaries Edward Everett Hale and Harriet Beecher Stowe, her parents had removed themselves from the social order through their profession and much of Hale's writing, exemplified by stories such as "The Readville Stars" and "The Empress's Ring," contrasts the high life of European aristocrats with the homely realities of her middle class Boston home. Hale herself attended the Winsor school and tried her hand as a painter at the School of the Museum of Fine Arts, Boston. She began seeking publication at the age of eleven and enjoyed success in her twenties and thirties with publications in *Vogue, Harper's, McCall's* and *The New Yorker*. The name of the newspaper she wrote and published as a child, *Society Cat*, suggests both her distance from high society and her desire to emulate it, while Hale's stories and memoirs circle relentlessly around the subjects of class and social shame. This theme is most clearly articulated in Hale's 1942 novel *The Prodigal Women*. Although the protagonist is a member of a Boston Brahmin family, her class position, like Hale's own, is complicated by her parents' relative poverty and her father's unstable status as an artist. Her social position, in fact, looks back to the struggling *petit bourgeois* heroines of *Little Women*, and it is tempting to see an allusion to Alcott's novel in both the title *The Prodigal Women* and the name of Hale's protagonist—Leda March. However, if Leda's class position recalls the sentimental heroines of the nineteenth century, it also evokes the self-made men and women of naturalism at the turn of the century. In the novel's inciting incident, Leda attends the dreaded birthday party of Adele, a wealthy classmate. Lacking the funds to purchase an appropriate gift, she wraps a bar of fancy soap in tissue paper and hopes for the best. Upon opening the gift, the terrifying Adele insists that Leda should use the soap herself—thus doubling Leda's shame and repurposing the gift as an instrument of torture. "'Wouldn't you like to use it now, Leda—there's a bathroom right in there. You must be dirty after that horrible old taxicab. Leda came in a taxicab,' Adele informed the girls. They all laughed." [1] Later, when Adele puts her arm around Leda and talks of the adventures they will share, the stunned party guest is willing to forgive all. But just at this crucial moment of weakness, Adele returns to the punishing mode with the complaint that, in washing her hands, Leda forgot to clean her nails, which are still offensively dirty. "'You didn't get your nails clean when you washed your hands, Leda . . . Go upstairs and clean them, will you. It'll make me sick to have to look at them at the table.'" [2] This is a defining moment for Leda; after

---

[1] *The Prodigal Women* 7

[2] Ibid. 10

this point, she determines to become invulnerable to Adele and her ilk, disavowing her love of nature and solitude to fight for social dominance among her peers.

This scene resonates with a biographical sketch from *A New England Girlhood* in which Hale explains how she shed her childish enthusiasm for learning and began to experience "the dismay, the reluctance, the dread" of formal education. In her childhood, Hale attended a day school run by the English Miss Cavendish, and the adult writer recalls how "we small descendants of Revolutionary patriots" were forced to stand up and sing "God Save the King." [3] Through the humor of this image, Hale underscores the class hierarchy of education. Young Nancy's ambition is fueled by her desire to become a member of "The Brigade," an all-male honor society for children with high marks and "characteristics like honor, trustworthiness, responsibility." Using a technique familiar from her fiction, Hale encapsulates her own youthful success and failure in a single crushing incident. After striving for years to be chosen for admission to The Brigade, the young girl finally wins the honor she has coveted for so long. However, instead of experiencing the expected pride and satisfaction, she is plunged into a "shaming" moment when Miss Cavendish takes the ceremony as an opportunity to comment, not on her academic or personal achievements, but on her dirty fingernails: "'It's not to be taken lightly, you know, as the only girl,'—she said 'gel'—'you will appreciate your position. And now,' she said, turning my hand over in hers, 'go into the bathroom and wash those dirty fingernails and hands.'" [4] The parallel with the fictionalized scene in *The Prodigal Women* is striking. In both cases, it is the hand and especially the fingers that bear the telltale signs of class. Although no literal cause is specified, the symbolism evokes labor,

---

[3] *A New England Girlhood* 38

[4] Ibid. 44

the mark on the hands associated with the defilement of physical exertion. Knowing that Hale attempted, in her early adulthood, to become a painter, and that she felt in some way handicapped by her parents' position as artists, the correlation in this scene between dirt and paint is clear. Artists and, like them, writers, inhabit an inherently conflicted class position because they must remain immured in their labor, however glorified or unalienated, in order to maintain their designated role as creative workers. The ascent to management by artists such as Thomas Kinkade or writers like James Frey may be lucrative, but even in our present age of corporate branding, it remains faintly absurd, a cultural contradiction in terms. Appropriately enough, the Brigade's motto is *"Fais Ce Que Tu Dois,"*—"Do What You Ought To," and as Nancy holds the honorary pin (pen?) in her hand, she feels, for the first time, the dual nature of ambition, which demands that one must stoop to conquer and embrace humiliation in order to succeed. Dipping her hands in the water and observing the pin through the distorting medium of the high glass shelf, she realizes, "I no longer wanted to be at school, I wanted to go home." [5]

Risk Management

The process that Nancy and Leda undergo may be understood in a Foucauldian sense, as the "productive" aspect of shame. Not only does such discipline create social subjects, it also produces art. Hale, determined from the age of eleven to publish and to publish well, understood, by the time she wrote *The Prodigal Women*, the cost of such shaming discipline, and her depiction of the unusual heroine Leda March is a testament to her deep contemplation of the subject. Unlike, say,

---

[5] *The Prodigal Women* 10

Becky Sharp (to whom one critic compares her), Leda does not "remake" herself in order to enact revenge on others, and unlike Jane Eyre, she does not succeed through proud Christian resistance and the plot machinations of the author. Rather, Leda allows herself to be shaped by shame while retaining a shadow sense, throughout the novel, of those portions of her consciousness sacrificed to the social order.

On first glancing at the book's title, a reader may anticipate a story about fallen women; in fact, this implication of sexual sin and redemption could account for the pulp appeal of this best-selling novel. But after a moment's consideration, we will remember that the moral implication of "prodigal" is gleaned largely from the Biblical story of the Prodigal Son, and that the word's literal meaning has more to do with wealth management than sexual transgression. The first definition of "prodigal" is "recklessly spendthrift," then, more positively, "luxuriant or yielding abundantly." (We should not, in our analysis, forget the other words that share the common root, such as "prodigious" and "prodigy.") Hale's female characters certainly break a number of sexual taboos. However, unlike the heroines of sentimental novels, they survive and indeed thrive, in spite of their excess of sexual, spiritual, economic, and interpersonal generosity. They have substance to spare. To be prodigal, for these women, is a measure of their strength, just as, I will argue, Hale's excess production, both in quantity and in the particular loose, reiterative and naturalistic form of *The Prodigal Women*, speaks to the robust nature of her artistic vocation. To be prodigal is to resist the shrinking reflex of shame.

In *The Program Era*, Mark McGurl identifies shame as the underlying motivation for post World War II fiction, particularly that fiction produced in university creative writing programs. Following Helen Murrell Lund's argument in *On Shame and the Search for Identity*, McGurl posits that shame, the fear of exposure to negative judgments, has replaced guilt, the remorse for transgressive acts, as the primary motivation in modern life. Further refining Lund's definition, he specifies that shame is "an emotion associated with involuntary subjection to social forces," such that an individual is continually vulnerable to unexpected exposure and the resulting sense of existential threat." [6] Because of increased geographical and class mobility in the second half of the twentieth century, subjects became ever more likely to experience rapid shifts of social context, thus risking further exposure and the attendant real or imagined negative judgment. However, as early as Hale's 1942 novel, significantly before the advent of the program era, shame appears to have replaced guilt as the dominant threat in social life. In fact, one shock for the contemporary reader of *The Prodigal Women* is the lack of guilt Hale's characters express, either internally or externally, for such acts as abortion, adultery, divorce, and promiscuity. Hale's work, after the fashion of the naturalists, removes the moral questions entirely in order to concentrate on environment, causality, sexuality, and the Darwinian drive for dominance and survival. If we want an image of a culture of shame, we need look no further than Leda or Nancy's dirty fingernails as the girls pass from the home environment of engaged artistic endeavor to the rarified abstraction of the school.

Shame is also the cornerstone in McGurl's discussion of "lower middle class modernism," a term he coins to describe the minimalist fictions fostered in creative writing programs and epitomized in the work of Raymond Carver. Such work rejects the form and subject matter of genre but also the experimentation and classical allusions of the avant-garde, using the compression associated with modernism to transform the

---

[6] *The Program Era* 285

raw material of shame into cultural capital. McGurl writes, "Minimalism had very little to say about emotion. That's because it was engineered as a way, not of explaining, but of beautifying shame." [7] McGurl contrasts the minimalism of Carver with the maximalism of Joyce Carol Oates, a contemporary who refused to "get with the program" and who has suffered, as a result, from a diminished literary reputation, in spite of her many publications and awards. Both writers began in underprivileged class positions, and as such, come to represent, for McGurl, the way in which the lower middle class was absorbed into the schools and disciplined into literary production. Carver, the successful program writer, learned to craft his class shame into miniature works of "risk management." Oates, however (at least in McGurl's analysis), rose to prominence and class privilege so quickly that she never learned to discipline herself, refusing to internalize or beautify shame. Instead, Oates over-produced, published uncategorizable works in many forms, and neglected to police her boundaries against genre, middlebrow, and women's fiction. As a result, she developed a feminized reputation as a prolific and overly fecund writer. Thus Oates represents, not shame, but "the pride of the unalienated literary laborer, articulating a limitless self from the raw material of body, memory, and text." [8] We might say, then, that Oates is a prodigal writer, and as such, her career speaks to the twin dilemmas of Leda March and Nancy Hale.

The Prodigal Women is more closely linked with naturalism and with mid-century women's novels such as Mary McCarthy's *The Group*. Dreiser too has been mentioned in connection with this work, but I also thought of D. H. Lawrence's *Women in Love*, or *The Rainbow* because of the in-depth analysis

---

[7] Ibid. 294

[8] Ibid. 312

of class, emotions, sexual relations, and the intricately drawn development of relationships over time. In any case, Hale's novel presents a sharp contrast to her short stories, even those written during the same time period and collected in *Between the Dark and the Daylight* the following year. In essence, then, Hale is both a minimalist and a maximalist, and as such, demonstrates within her own body of work the distinction McGurl draws between Carver and Oates, shame and pride, compression and expansion. In her stories, Hale evokes shame, creating suggestive but enigmatic mosaics out of the broken icons of class signifiers. But in *The Prodigal Women*, she does what McGurl says a good lower middle class modernist should never do, by taking shame as her explicit theme and attempting to examine its sources and effects.

From the initial shaming of Leda March, we can trace the entire outline of the book. Leda, after her traumatic encounter with Adele, sets out to evade shame, to perform the real world equivalent of the literary "risk management" that McGurl attributes to Carver. She does so, largely through social manipulations, convincing her parents to let her leave the Country Day School for Miss Sheraton's superior establishment, enlisting the aid of her Aunt March to launch her career as a debutante, and marrying her cousin James, who represents a significant rise in social and economic status. However, she does engage, tangentially, with artistic and educational goals. At school, she begins to read and write poetry and is mentored by a serious and inelegant teacher who encourages her to apply for a scholarship. But Leda, intent upon conquering the social system, disdains the literary life as the "easy path." Besides, if she wants to avoid detection, she needs to keep her hands clean.

Shame is also investigated through the secondary story line about the Jekyll family, especially the sisters Betsy and Maizie, who will serve as foils for and occasional rivals to Leda March.

The Jekyll's primary function, in Leda's early development, is to provide a shame-free space, a disorderly and happy household where Leda can find a respite from the hierarchy and disapproval of the Boston social scene. This shamelessness is associated with the Jekyll's status as Southerners. To be a Southerner, in Hale's primitivist paradigm, is to be freed of social shame.

The shamelessness of the Jekylls however, extends beyond the regionalist pattern to embrace the shame of the female body. George Herbert Clarke complained about Hale's insistence, in this novel, on physical passion rather than "the true spirit of love." [9] However, in retrospect, this is one of the most compelling elements of the work. In *The Prodigal Women*, one character undergoes a risky abortion in order to please her husband. Another, in the course of her career in New York, engages with multiple sexual partners, while married and unmarried, and feels no remorse. In fact, her conscience remains so pristine that her second husband, a Catholic writer, feels compelled to try to "discipline" her into the proper attitude of shame at her own sexual past. Finally, Leda herself finds her greatest happiness in an adulterous relationship conducted, significantly, in Virginia. This frank portrayal of women's sexual experiences in the '20s and '30s is one of the novel's greatest appeals for a contemporary reader. Not only is the treatment of these transgressions incredibly explicit, but the women are not forced to "pay" for their experiences. Or, rather, their only punishment appears to be the abuse of male characters, who, in spite of their valiant efforts, never fully succeed in forcing their prodigal women to internalize the patriarchal taboos regarding female sexuality. All three women survive their sexual transgressions and live to experience some degree of peace or happiness. Strikingly, the only suicide in the novel is that of the Jekyll father, who cannot endure his

---

[9] Clarke 2

exile in the North and the shame of his daughter's promiscuity and his wife's desertion.

The Jekyll shamelessness contrasts with Leda's cultivation of a life shaped to perfection by shame. After exploiting the benefits of the Jekyll family, Leda moves on to her next teacher, a conventional young woman who makes the most irregular arrangements seem perfectly normal. Leda, under the influence of this normalizing force, decides to marry her cousin in spite of her aversion to the "boredom" he represents. However, in the meantime, she indulges in an unconsummated affair with Lambert, an artist and the husband of Maizie Jekyll. Lambert, though a disastrous and indeed abusive match for Maizie, provides Leda with the only positive sexual connection of her life. He endears himself to her, first of all, by commenting on the fatal flaw of her old enemy Adele, whose "fat legs" he omits from the portrait he is painting of her. By shaming Adele, he aligns himself with Leda, who has by now remade herself into an irreproachable beauty. However, when Leda realizes the scandal to which this affair exposes her, she retreats back into her engagement and eventual marriage to James. Only after her divorce will she return to Lambert and a renewed interest in poetry and the arts.

The Sea, the Scene

In an intriguing collection of what we would now call craft essays on the art of writing, Hale describes the distinction between short story and novel with a lovely and incisive metaphor:

> It is possible to think of the novel as one great body of water, a lake perhaps. The crests of its waves are the scenes, in which characters speak, move, reveal, act; the troughs of the waves connecting them are the transition passages, also revealing, explaining, disclosing, informing, all the while that they are stealth-

ily—unnoticed by all but the unusually suspicious—moving the reader on and up to the crest of the succeeding wave.[10]

This memorable image goes a long way toward describing Hale's own fiction. In *The Prodigal Women*, the troughs tend to delineate the social mores first of Boston society, then of débutante and bohemian culture. Other passages relate directly to nature, especially Leda March's perceptions of the woods surrounding her home. The scenes, then, rising from these rills of summary, have a quality of being in time and in context. One of the most striking is Betsy's experience of childbirth. I choose this example because it has literally to do with the sea. After an evening of being verbally abused by her intoxicated husband, Betsy goes into labor and, reluctant to wake her sleeping spouse and ask for his help, she walks to the home of a neighbor who then rows her across the bay to the hospital. This is perhaps the most shameful experience of embodiment in the novel. Helpless, abandoned by her husband, forced to walk door to door to enlist aid, Betsy would, in most stories, find herself in the depths of despair. But Hale's representation of her character's consciousness at this moment gives the impression of the most dramatic strength.

> The pains came regularly, increasing in the range of their thoroughness, but there was none of them that quite blacked out the sea…The feeling she had between the pains was one of earned release and a strange comfortable enjoyment. It was as though she were aware in her whole self of the current discharge of all duty. She feared nothing. Everything had been accounted for…In this world everything was in its place. It was a world as snug and self-contained as an orange…. In the spaces between her pains she was left free, really free with the conscienceless freedom of a child to enjoy freedom.[11]

---

[10] *The Realities of Fiction* 43-44

[11] *The Prodigal Women* 488-9

In this passage, Betsy moves beyond social shame toward the pain, the sea, the physical universe. She does so not by rejecting the solid facts of class or body or sexuality or even by struggling against an abusive husband. Instead, she practices a form of radical acceptance. I would argue that it is, in part, the loose, naturalistic, and full-bodied methodology of the novel that allows Hale to depict this moment of altered reality, the character bound to time and place, and yet also engaged with timelessness. The fragmentary modernist story, painfully compressed, cut off from summary and context, often produces a pleasing frisson of ambiguity. However, that fragmentary representation, so powerful when practiced by Hemingway or Anderson, can too easily become rigid, reified like a mosaic made of broken icons. Hale's stories have some of this rigidity, and it is this sense of cold perfection and limit to which her critics often respond.

Hale herself was enamored of the sea, and describes her anticipation, each summer, of her visit to the beach and the bucket and shovel she would receive upon arriving at her aunt's home. There is, in this description, some intimation of the writer's attitude toward her vocation: the tiny container and the vast ocean. In Hale's stories, she makes impressive use of the shovel and bucket to create well-fashioned sand castles for the market, but in *The Prodigal Women*, she delves into larger bodies of water and opens a passageway to the sea.

The Prodigal Women offers unexpected pleasures for contemporary readers. It depicts female experience, particularly sexual experience of the '20s and '30s, in ways that have not been incorporated into the literary canon. One of the characters has an illegal and botched abortion; another combines a career as a writer and model for a women's magazine with a promiscuous lifestyle; a third lives openly with a married man after her divorce. Formally, too, the book presents an original and compelling pattern. Using a third person limited point-of-view, Hale alternates between her three female protagonists, Leda March and the sisters Maizie and Betsy Jekyll. The strategy is not overtly experimental, as in the work of, say, Virginia Woolf. However, Hale's movement from one protagonist to the next, linear but irregular, enacts a deeply organic organization of multiple interrelated storylines. Plot points create natural breaks, and when these occur, Hale moves from one character to the next, often without any formal acknowledgement of the shift in perspective. So, for example, when Leda March goes to visit her aunt and uncle for the summer, the narrative opens up to accommodate Maizie Jekyll's ill-fated romance with Lambert. It looks, at this point, as if we are experiencing a disruptive shift. But later, when Leda becomes involved with Lambert herself, the plotting assumes a thematic significance, alongside the sheerly formal dramatic structure. Breaks are not formally noted, and have the effect of overlapping leaves. In addition, the novel is asymmetrical; the sections are of vastly varying lengths, ranging from a few pages of Betsy's perspective to over one hundred in the case of Maizie, who, up until this point, had appeared to be a minor character. Although Leda, whose narrative opens and concludes the novel and whose story is more obviously a *bildungsroman*, appears to be the protagonist, her friends the Jekyll sisters are given nearly as much space. By this device, Hale interrogates the individualistic portrayal of the singular heroine and suggests that the characters exist in relationship to one another. Hale's elegant plotting is both modular and architectural. That is, the character's stories, presented side by side, suggest parallels and evoke questions about the alternate paths open to women. But the novel also works chronologically and causally, since Maizie's husband will be the same figure as Leda's lover and the two stories depend upon that relation in time and space. Hale's plotting develops narrative suspense alongside existential anticipation, for instance, toward the end of the novel, we get an extensive scene of Betsy's marriage, all the while wondering when our protagonist Leda will reappear and solve the enigma of her own romantic entanglement.

The School of Shame

The Prodigal Women functions not only as a *Bildungsroman* of female development, but also as a gloss on the artistic practices of the period between the wars, and it poses the question of how to develop an artistic practice in the face of shame. Interestingly, Hale deflects this artistic ambition onto her male characters, the artist Lambert and the writer Hector. Both men are deeply conflicted about their artistic goals, and both blame the women in their lives for their inability to work up to their potential. Lambert blames first Maizie's pregnancy, then the illness that follows upon her botched abortion, entailing large doses of enforced rest, which he considers directly opposed to the artistic life of action. Hector blames his wife Betsy's former promiscuity, which absorbs his thoughts, threatens his ego, and interferes with the production of his book. For me, part of the pleasure of the novel resides in Hale's rich, frank, and honest portrayal of the lives of the wives of artists in the period of high modernists Hemingway and Stein. Unlike Stein, however, Hale focuses her attention on the wives of would-be geniuses, showing the trials (an abortion in South America, a public display of infidelity, labor without the benefit of transportation to the hospital because the artist husband has passed out in an alcoholic stupor) attendant upon life with artists. Hale's portrayal of Lambert and Hector also speaks to the shame of the artist who has betrayed the romantic life of the bohemian to enter into the bonds of domesticity, aligning himself, in the process, with the female body. Hale uses internal summary to reveal the habitual state of Hector's turmoil:

> It was like madness, to wonder what she thought; he
> seemed to feel a real fever mounting in his blood. His life
> was wrecked, his work remained undone, while this streak
> of poison ran through his strength like a streak in granite.
> A tap, and the stone falls apart. The fever mounted, and
> he had the terror that his life would never be collected
> again; she had foundered it and split it upon the fact of her
> past. . . ." [12]

In fact, Lambert and Hector have been lucky to find the
accommodating Jekyll sisters, who feel no need to repress their
sexuality and who seem to lack any desire for wealth or social
standing. However, the very physical fact of their femininity
is cause for their artist-husbands to feel shame. The domestic
scenes between these two couples, textbook portrayals of gendered emotional abuse, make for painful reading. However, it
is one of the virtues of the novel to show how such intense
emotional violence can be normalized through marriage.
Again, for the men as well as for the women, the female body
is itself the subject of shame, that which represents what cannot be absorbed into the social order or the aesthetic sphere.

Leda, who has managed to avoid passion of both the physical and the artistic variety in pursuit of social invulnerability,
makes another test case for the artist. Hale denies her protagonist the artistic fulfillment that she herself experienced. In
fact, it is the secondary character Betsy, a writer and occasional
model for a women's magazine in New York, whose career
bears the closest biographical resemblance to Hale's own. But
Betsy has no particular aspirations beyond escaping Boston
and having a good time. Leda is the only female character who
appears to long for some artistic expression. Leda, whose life

---

[12] *The Prodigal Women* 473

work consists of protecting herself from social exposure, never totally devotes herself to art, and yet her intermittent returns to the practice of poetry mark her moments of greatest happiness. Hale includes passages of Leda's poetry, and these are often difficult to read, since their literary quality is not as polished or professional as the surrounding prose narration:

> Chary of trust
> And afraid of love
> We believe in dust
> Below and above…
> Until we are shown
> We cannot believe.
> We have never known what it is to grieve
> For someone else.
> We are racked with sorrow
> Because today melts
> Into tomorrow.[13]

The insistent regular rhymes evoke a kind of plodding monotony and the specter of amateur verse. And yet, if we read the summary, the sea from which these verses arise, we get a much fuller account of their significance:

> [S]he would put the books down on the floor and pick up the pad of paper and the pencil and begin to write what flowed into her mind, and it seemed as if now, in these days, everything was made clear and articulate. All that in ordinary life was matter of fact, obscure, and complicated was now resolved; she seemed to know the answer to things which in life she did not know the answer to. The people she had known, the events which she had observed, from being meaningless became significant and she could express them in a pattern. From this shell of comprehension where she was curled she could view her own and other people's

---

[13] Ibid. 422

confusion and express it. All the years in New York which she had cast off now took on their value.[14]

The "shell of contemplation," another provocative image associated with Hale's love of the sea, can be taken as an aesthetic assertion, not to value the literary product as a fetish object but as a means to contemplation and comprehension. This is the opposite of the "risk management" Leda has been practicing in her social life, maximizing her prestige by withholding her sentiments from those around her. Here, Hale is also turning away from the "risk management" practiced in her stories and sketches for *The New Yorker*. There is a kind of courage in letting these lines stand as they are, not to mark Leda as a prodigy or genius, but simply an individual for whom artistic endeavor is a relief from the social pressures of hierarchy. By the end of the novel, this desire to write has been subsumed into a general desire to live, and the poetry has been integrated into Leda's internal monologue: "To be at peace; to be alone; to be myself. To feel the splendid wave sweep silent over noise, the coming down, the overwhelming, beautiful with a thousand silent voices." [15]

Some might see the conclusion of *The Prodigal Women* as a disheartening one. Maizie's marriage ends, Betsy remains with her verbally abusive husband, and Leda gives up custody of her son. However, we leave none of these prodigal women in a state of despair. Rather, their prodigal nature has taught them to open up to experience and to the deeper sea running beneath socially defined reality. But it is quite distinct from the naturalism of Dreiser in that it shows the process of characters working through their circumstances and toward some existential awareness of their position in and outside of time. Hale's characters

---

[14] Ibid. 422
[15] Ibid. 555

remain rooted in their circumstances and their social positions. And yet, unlike most of the protagonists of naturalism, they are not defeated by their environment. Instead, something in this method allows these prodigal women, and the reader with them, to connect to a place beyond shame, into an acceptance of the sheer physical facts of embodiment, sexuality, and imperfection.

To return to McGurl, one wonders whether the "prodigal" nature of Hale's bestselling novel and of her writing career in general has harmed her reputation as a literary novelist. Certainly her career bears some resemblance to Oates's, since over a lifetime, she produced a large body of work—over thirty volumes in various genres such as short stories, novels, memoirs, and biography—and because that work has been relegated from time to time to the realm of "women's writing." *The Prodigal Woman* has the appeal of much of Oates's fiction—the historical sweep, the verbal facility, the sexual frankness, the elegant movement from interiority to external action and summary to scene. Further it shares Oates's thematic emphasis on class position and the attendant shame of involuntary subjection to social forces.

The Prodigal Women fills an important gap in several ways: its unsanitized treatment of women's sexuality in that brief period of openness between the world wars, its woman-centered perspective on the bohemian life of the artist, its development of a fluid, organic, and yet highly formal plot structure, its unique hybrid of modernism and naturalism at a moment just before the program era and the twin trends of postmodernism and minimalism, and finally, its highly articulated treatment of shame, perhaps the defining theme of literary fiction in the second half of the twentieth century.

Hale's career, located just before the explosion of the program era, can also help us reflect on the state of the creative writing industry, as we now call it without hesitation. What is the cost of shaming and disciplining our students into submission to a code of lower middle class modernism? What is repressed by such relentless packaging of the self? What is the personal cost of "risk management" in the act of aestheticizing and fetishizing one's class position, one's race or ethnicity, one's sexual orientation or gender oppression? What works might be produced out of shamelessness? I will never forget one moment in a writing workshop, where a classmate and friend was publically "shamed" for her work because it accessed sexuality, class sensibility, and feminist rage. My own story, safely ensconced, like the most highly praised of Hale's stories, in the pre-sexual world of childhood, and rooted in the modernist values of containment, stoicism, and impersonality, was awarded universal approval. As a writing teacher, I return to that moment again and again, hoping that I will not reproduce it. The problem with the workshop, from my perspective, is not so much that it is a school—for the collective urge toward enlightenment is surely a worthy impulse—but that it is a school of shame. Here we encourage students to "master" their traumas by packaging them in airless prose, with the maximum number of verbal "gems" per page (or stanza, as the case may be). As a result, this trauma itself is fetishized. If suffering is what we value, what gives us our identity and brings us social prestige, we tend to dwell in that suffering to set it up as an idol and commodity. What might happen if instead, we followed Leda March in regarding the literary artifact as the shell of comprehension from which some larger understanding might emerge?

Works Cited

Clarke, George Herbert. "Women Interpret Women." *Virginia Quarterly Review*. 1943. Web, May 2010.

Hale, Nancy. *Between the Dark and the Daylight*. New York: Charles Scribner's Son's, 1943.

—————. *The Empress's Ring*. Boston & Toronto: Little Brown and Company, 1958.

—————. *A New England Girlhood*. Boston: Little, Brown and Company, 1936.

—————. *The Realities of Fiction: A Book About Writing*. Boston, Toronto: Little, Brown and Company, 1961.

Larcom, Lucy. *A New England Girlhood*. Gloucester, Mass: Peter Smith, 1973.

McGurl, Mark. *The Program Era: Postwar Fiction and the Rise of Creative Writing*. Cambridge, Mass & London: Harvard University Press, 2009.

TRUDY LEWIS is the author of a short story collection, *The Bones of Garbo* (Ohio State University Press, 2003), for which she was awarded the Sandstone Prize in Short Fiction, and a novel, *Private Correspondences* (Northwestern University Press, 1994), winner of the William Goyen Award for Fiction. Lewis's work has appeared in *Atlantic Monthly, Best American Short Stories, Chelsea, Fence, Five Points, Iris, Meridian, New England Review, New Stories from the South, Third Coast, Witness*, and others.

Nancy Hale and Feminism:
on *The Prodigal Women*

Norah Hardin Lind

Nancy Hale's bestseller of 1942, *The Prodigal Women*, attracted attention with its daring revelations about the significantly shifting role of women during the 1920s and the 1930s. The novel provides a cultural study of the complex social period when women emerged from the cocoon of Victorian restrictions to become valuable members of society. Hale consistently captured the universal moments of life through the vivid descriptions in her short stories. This lengthy third novel proved for the first time that she was capable of performing her magic on a larger stage with fully developed characters. The narrative follows the interwoven lives of three women who, freed from the traditional burdens of domesticity, make life decisions, but Hale's women do not always choose well. Mary Lee Settle's introduction to the 1988 reprint of *The Prodigal Women* reveals Hale's own thoughts about the novel's huge success:

> At the time it was first published, the honest sexuality of the book obscured both the structure and the characters, according to Nancy Hale. People tended to read it for its shock value. To a reader today that aspect of it seems very mild. Now, over forty years later, the sexuality can be taken for granted and admired for its honest picture of what life was, and is, like for a woman.[1]

---

[1] Settle xi

Settle correctly recognizes the significance of Hale's work as a chronicle of the values and behaviors of the people of a period.[2] The three main characters all demonstrate aspects of the author, even as a gender reading of *The Prodigal Women* reveals universal conflicts confronting women of the period in terms of social and sexual freedoms which led to new positions in the workplace.[3]

In *The Prodigal Women* Nancy Hale interwove the freedoms of the period's New Woman with the structures that they were replacing, which did not simply cease to exist when women emerged from the kitchen. Hale described her own approach as individual, not a part of a social movement. Reporter Guy Friddell wrote that Hale believed the women's liberation movement had to happen; she described it as "a spontaneous expression that had to come up. Much of it is carried to such extremes that it defeats itself; but then you can't hoist something out of a morass unless you go to extremes."[4] Hale's narrative often expresses the extremes of the turbulent period.

The women in Nancy Hale's narrative react individually to the new age. In 1980 Hale's friend Anne Freeman wrote of *The Prodigal Women*:

> Through these three radically different women, Nancy Hale dramatizes three responses to the age-old problem of being a woman—of trying to establish a separate identity and if possible acquire a modicum of power, yet still fulfill that

---

[2] Ibid. vii

[3] Swinth, Kirsten: *Painting professionals. Women Artists and the Development of Modern American Art, 1870–1930*. Kirsten Swinth describes the women who had emerged: "The most radical of the New Women embraced sexual liberation and female economic independence—the two beliefs that most shaped the new movement called feminism. In the name of all women, feminism validated the full development of female selfhood and, significantly, the pursuit of individual aims" (169).

[4] Friddell

vague, transcendent, biological pull into motherhood and its ensuing complications. It is the problem the New Feminists would be analyzing endlessly some thirty years after *The Prodigal Women* came out. [5]

The decade leading up to writing the book laid the groundwork for *The Prodigal Women*. Nancy Hale and Taylor Hardin had moved to New York City after marrying in the fall of 1928. Although she was only twenty, Hale slid smoothly into the literary life of New York. Youthful career-seekers, rebounding from war's incongruous message about life's uncertainty, pursued a level of hedonism that America had never experienced. Hale had already written of the zeitgeist in her first novel, *The Young Die Good*, published when she was twenty six. It describes the complete freedom of the era and the subsequent lack of stability. Hale's characters are fascinated by New York and the unconventional. The novel was not as well received as her later work, but it captures the spirit of the city:

> New York is perhaps after all, only the circus that it has so often been compared to. It is a very good circus, very complete. It is a little too good. There is no time in any one's life to see all that this circus offers. When you come in to the circus you are blinded by lights and deafened by the shouts of the barkers. You are curious of what you will see in the inviting side-shows. What you see there may be amusing, perhaps shocking and perhaps only revolting. What I would say, however, is that if you listen to the adjectives thrown at you by all the barkers, if you go in to all the side-shows, you will inevitably miss the big lion act and the important tight-rope walking that are what you really came to see. Your only chance is to put your mind firmly upon what you came to the circus to witness, and to ignore the fat lady and the sword swallower and the dreadful blue man, and go directly to your seat in the main tent. You may

---

[5] Freeman 214

be too early and have to sit and wait for the show, but when it is over you will have seen the circus, the real circus that is a great and exciting sight, and not merely have bewildered and even nauseated yourself with the strange spectacles in the side-shows.[6]

New York City witnessed a faltering cultural hegemony as the younger generation moved in a destructive and hedonistic direction from the domination of the conservative remnants of Victorianism. Nancy Hale describes vividly the youthful views which echo the debauchery and void of social conscience that Fitzgerald popularized in *The Great Gatsby*. She had confronted existing social restrictions already in her short stories. "Club Car," the first of approximately eighty Nancy Hale stories published by *The New Yorker*, is an open confrontation of past values. A young career woman is forced by the lateness of her travel planning to take a train that the narrator condemns, speaking of it like an unpopular member of an industrial social order: "It was not an extra-fare train. It was not even one of those quiet, self-respecting trains that make their New York-to-Boston trip in a consistent five-and-a-half hours. It was just an unassuming old train that didn't pretend to take less than six hours, and really took seven. . . ." [7] The car is cold and unpleasant, filled with traveling matrons and children. Dissatisfied with the accommodations, the young woman shifts into the club car where she lights a cigarette. The club car is more pleasant; it is the world reserved for men. She quickly senses that she is not welcome here: "I became aware that I was doing something that wasn't done. I became aware that, thoroughly depraved through contact with dissolute extra-fare trains, I had violated a sanctuary. I had come into the club car, and I was a woman." [8] The

---

[6] *The Young Die Good* 51-2

[7] "The Club Car" 42

[8] Ibid. 43

narrator recognizes with discomfort that the other occupants of the car, all male, see her as a seductress, a woman of ill morals. Nonetheless, intent upon finishing her cigarette, she selects a seat. She smokes companionably opposite a middle-aged gentleman, until she notices that he has scribbled a message to her on the window: "I am married."[9] She returns to her rightful place in the cold car filled with women and children.

This episode of trespass on the male world addresses the conflicts caused by shifting standards for women. Messages signaled that women who smoked were trashy and promiscuous, yet a barrage of advertising encouraged them to take up the habit. The August 26, 1933 issue of *The New Yorker* contains a Camel cigarette advertisement picturing a bejeweled, feminine hand removing a filterless cigarette from the pack offered by a well-groomed, masculine hand. The copy reads, "Camels are made from finer, MORE EXPENSIVE tobaccos than any other popular brand."[10] The ad clearly targets a female audience, and it acknowledges that the brand of the cigarettes offered is as important as the flavor of food. Hale represents the smoking conflict in "Club Car" with its juxtaposition of old and new, Victorian and modern. The women on the train are confined by their maternal roles, while the young, free-thinking narrator asserts woman's new position in the modern age. Hale may have found inspiration for the narrative from her involvement in a renowned advertising campaign of 1929. Women smokers of the 1920s were a matter of social consternation, provoking a counter-attacking crusade by American Tobacco Company to encourage female smoking. The progressive advertising campaign called *Torches of Freedom* employed a behavioral approach, which equated female smoking with powerful, elite role models. Aiming to change the image of women smokers from degener-

---

[9] Ibid. 43

[10] *The New Yorker* 5

ate to emancipated, the campaign provided a repetitious associ-
ation between cigarettes and freedoms formerly withheld from
women. Eddie Bernays, the advertising wizard who engineered
the offensive, matched the desires of the women of the period
with the product he represented. The nephew of Sigmund
Freud, Bernays spearheaded the use of psychological tactics in
advertising. Bernays understood that the taboo against smoking
was a gender construct geared to equate smoking with a breach
in morality; his goal was to reveal such social manipulations as
repressive for women. The new Bernays equation publicized images of elite role models smoking to reverse the negative public
perception of the behavior. The *Torches of Freedom* campaign focused on debutante-types who occupied enviable social positions
like Nancy Hale Hardin, the name she used socially. A prominent
photograph in the campaign shows the attractive young Hardins
strolling down Fifth Avenue. She carries her torch of freedom
while her husband's cigarette is clenched jauntily between his
lips.

Bernays endorsed the modern attitude against restrictions
on women's behavior. His advertisements linked New York's
society women in the act of smoking, with the concept of social
freedom. Nancy Hale viewed the publicity stunt as a way to
make money. She wrote to her mother that she had received
$10 for appearing in a photograph, and she had been offered
the potential for far greater sums in the future. Later, she wrote
of receiving more money from the ad campaign: "$100 for sign-
ing my name to some sort of letter they are going to send to
the editors of magazines asking them to give the idea of smoking on the street publicity, and I have a tentative agreement with
them that if there is sufficient publicity I am to receive $1000
for endorsing an advertisement [. . . .] Pretty soft way to make
money, isn't it?" [11] Her comment identifies Hale as the product

---

[11] NHP, SSC, 6.8

of an era rather than as a spokeswoman for change. The *Torches of Freedom* campaign targeted the New Woman, and Nancy Hale was its bellwether. The changing environment included a constant flow of consumer products reflecting the new mobility for women with its undercurrent of sexuality.[12] *A Century of Women* surveys the changes affecting women during the twentieth century; Sheila Rowbotham writes that a "barrage of propaganda from advertisers presented American women with vision of personal freedom. . . ." [13]

Smoking was one of many social rules that women were challenging. Their hair styles and fashions altered as well; they drank in speakeasies, and their sexual behavior shifted to echo a traditionally masculine approach. This was a shocking departure from the feminine virtue that previous eras had maintained. The three prodigals of Hale's novel demonstrate all of the mannerisms of the New Woman. Through them, Hale relates the story of her second marriage, but legendary editor Maxwell Perkins assured the author of her novel's amplified significance as a cultural document: "I think your book is really much bigger and better than even the best reviewers realized. It tells much that never was before revealed. And the business of literature is to reveal life. Not, of course, in just the realistic sense, for it is done by the poets too, and in fact what underlies your writing is a poet." [14]

Perkins offered continual support to Hale as she struggled to translate reality into fiction, and *The Prodigal Women* brought Scribner's the profits to justify its support of Hale during her first two less lucrative books. Hale struggled with this novel, and she wrote to William Maxwell, whom she called "a kind

---

[12] Rowbotham describes aspects of the period in terms of the daily life for women (161-171).

[13] Rowbotham 161

[14] Perkins 209

of artistic conscience"[15]: "The whole scale is so big and you have to keep your mind on the big side, the whole picture, and somehow you can't also write in careful detail; I mean you can't write the kind of accurate smell-and-sound stuff that I know I can sometimes do well, but must write on a larger, looser scale of which I am unsure since I have no experience with it. I hope to God it turns out right. I know the book is about something important (to me) and that the parts are right to tell the bigger story. . . ."[16] Despite what she felt to be a lack of sensory detail, committing the memories of her broken second marriage to paper required a painful revisiting of emotions, which led Hale to a nervous breakdown after the release of the novel. Not only did the material of the novel break new ground, but Hale's friend Jungian analyst John Beebe said, in a personal interview, that the style of her writing was fresh as well, "She was ahead of her time in personal memoir—not fiction. Confessional literature emerged in the 60s; Nancy Hale was flirting with that form years before—flirting with the intersection between fiction and memoir. She writes nonfiction short stories ahead of Capote. She is doing more than describe the outer event—she includes what is happening in the mind as well."

The Prodigal Women was an immediate success; Hale reaped the profits from the sale of millions of copies of the book, along with an additional $25,000 for the movie rights. Her characters find a world beyond the kitchen as they battle men emotionally. The men, in reaction, assert their dominance, controlling and threatening the female characters. The account is frightening in its violence; Anne Freeman writes that it "dramatized, with unflinching candor, the psychological cost of being a woman at that time."[17] Hale opens *The Prodigal Women*

---

[15] 1943 letter , NHP, SSC, 14.20

[16] NHP, SSC, 14.20

[17] Freeman 214

with a moment of tragic social exclusion. It is the universal type of experience that appears frequently in Hale's works, calling the audience into the narrative. Young Leda March attends the birthday party of a Boston schoolmate. She is filled both with anguish for the shunning that she expects and with hope that this time will be different, and she will feel a part of things, emotions that the audience shares. Her fears prove well-founded; the party is a disaster. Hale's decision to launch her novel around the concept of social "otherness" proves appropriate, for the massive work is a study of the outsider in various forms, all of them female, each struggling for position and power. The social situation which favored men on every level—in the home, and in business, educational, and legal areas—led feminists to conceive the term sexism. *The Prodigal Women* describes the difficulties young women encountered confronting these biases, ill prepared by their conservative childhoods to cope with their new freedom. It is a story of domination and subordination as the three women battle stereotypically powerful and aggressive males, confronting issues which would not be discussed openly for two more decades.

The immediate acceptance of Hale's explicit novel indicates the public spirit favoring change. During World War I women had replaced men in the work force and had begun to recognize and to appreciate their own abilities as workers. The world of women who checked their faces in mirrors and worried if their dance cards were full had been revised, and *The Prodigal Women* speaks forthrightly of a new desire for freedom and personal fulfillment. The protagonists are overtly sexual and defiant of the code of conduct that they long had been forced to adopt.

----

[18] Hale's fictional account confronts issues that Kate Millett discusses in her powerful and influential feminist treatise of 1968, *Sexual Politics*. Millett's appraisal of the patriarchical society which had long forced women into submission is the same hovering element of fear that governs the actions of Hale's characters.

Unlike earlier literary representations of women, Hale's characters are not bound to the domestic world; they are often on the move, pursuing careers. The three women smoke, drink, and enjoy sex without marriage. The protagonists make their own choices; they are not all strong; they do not always win their battles against men. Too often they subjugate personal desires to masculine demands, highlighting the turmoil which accompanied the era's shift in mores coupled with the need to find a replacement for the structures of the past.

The Prodigal Women revolves around the relationships of Leda March, a New England native, and two sisters who have just moved to Boston from Virginia. The younger sister, Betsy Jekyll, becomes Leda's closest childhood friend, and the beautiful, older sister, Maizie, is the object of their admiration. Maizie clings to her Southern views, describing her goals to her mother: "I don't care anything about all this marrying somebody important. Honestly, I don't. I just want to be happy. I just want to marry somebody I love." [19] Marriage begins as the path to her fulfillment, but it also brings her ruin. She becomes pregnant, and the object of her adoration, Lambert Rudd, must marry her. Hale continually opens Maizie's thoughts to the reader, as Lambert feels increasingly trapped. She relates that Maizie "knew what she wanted—for him to love her as a man should love a woman. It remained for her to find the ways to make him into that kind of man. She did not know them but they must exist, and, she thought, she would find them if it killed her." [20] Attempting to give Lambert Rudd what she believes he desires, Maizie finds an abortion doctor while on a cruise in South America. An infection results, and after a second surgery to save her life, Maizie is told not to have sexual relations with her husband for a

---

[19] *The Prodigal Women* 41

[20] Ibid. 69

month. He goes out alone in the evening and on returning, experiences her usual round of jealous questions. Rudd confesses that he has been with a girl and that he has kissed her, he says, "About five—small—kisses underneath a moon on a nightclub terrace." [21] Driven to keep her husband, Maizie compromises her health to provide the sexual relationship that he claims to require. Maizie finally has a child with Lambert, but she never regains her strength and lives for years in a sanitarium in her Southern home town, recovering from a nervous breakdown. The relationship with the forceful Rudd destroys the Southern girl who seeks a traditional marriage.

The second of Hale's prodigals is Betsy, Maizie's sister and Leda's close childhood friend. She experiences the restrictive Boston society when her father reacts to a conversation on the commuter train. Another businessman reports having seen Betsy leave a male's room alone, and her father arrives home exclaiming, "I'm not going to have my daughter a common prostitute. I'm not going to have a common Yankee bastard on a train telling me my daughter is a prostitute and laughing at me, the Yankee bastard...." [22] She rejects the suffocating New England atmosphere for the freedoms of New York City. Through Betsy, Nancy Hale describes the feelings and tastes of the developing persona of the New Woman: "Betsy felt as strong as ten men and her heart was as high as the air, and of all the places in the world there were to be in, she was glad to be here. She walked with long, vigorous steps on her high heels across the freshly watered streets in her new, smart little tweed dresses and her little hats. She knew she looked like a boy and she was glad; she felt like a boy. To be a young girl in New York in those days was to be like a young boy: as free, as unshackled, as adventurous." [23]

---

[21] Ibid. 77

[22] Ibid. 250

[23] Ibid. 280

Each of the three prodigal women embodies elements of Hale's own life. Betsy quickly lands a job on a fashion magazine called *Lady*; Hale worked on the staffs of *Vogue* and *Vanity Fair*. Hale filled in as a model when necessary, and she writes of Betsy: "In a pinch she might be sent to fill in at a sitting herself as a model. All the fashion assistants were chosen with an eye to their ability to pinch-hit as models. . . ." [24] Hale clearly equates the women with males:

> The girls were on as confident a footing as the men. The men had unlimited money; but they had unlimited youth, and were equals. They said what they pleased and did what they pleased, knowing that if one man did not like it there was another who would. With their long, boylike stride they walked into the Embassy Club, the Lido, the Broadway nightclubs with a floor the size of a handkerchief, the theatres, along the side-streets towards a taxi, into a hundred speakeasies on all the West and East streets near Fifth Avenue, hailing the bartenders, joking with the waiters, dancing, listening, talking with their cropped heads held high on their long necks, their broad shoulders hunched as they leaned on a speakeasy table, their hair bare when they pulled their hats off with a careless gesture in a restaurant; their hips narrow, their legs long. [25]

Betsy reveals how modern her ideas have become in a rhyme which she regrets reciting in front of pregnant sister Maizie: "There was an old woman who lived in a shoe/And had so many children she didn't know what to do./But there was a young woman who lived in a shoe,/And she didn't have any children, for she knew what to do." [26] The verse refers to the demand for birth control by radical groups of the 1920s. The knowledge that Betsy reveals in flippant rhyme is considered inappropriate by Maizie's husband and mother-in-law, who represent traditional thought.

---

[24] Ibid. 281

[25] Ibid. 284

[26] Ibid. 300

Hale does not leave Betsy to her exciting new career, instead introducing all the conflicts the New Women experience in reaction to their free behavior. Betsy falls in love with the writer Hector, who embodies the male characteristics described by Christine Stansell in *American Moderns: Bohemian New York and the Creation of a New Century*. Stansell describes the need for a vigorous, masculine character to squelch the threat posed by the New Woman.[27] Hale builds Hector as a demonic and abusive figure, determined to know about every sexual action in Betsy's past. The battle between old and new values is played out frighteningly in *The Prodigal Women* when Hector grills Betsy night after night to name her past lovers. His efforts to jog her memory, to break her down, are a brutally abusive demonstration of the double standard. She explains her life before meeting him:

"I wasn't a pushover. Can't you see? I always felt like a boy."
She is only behaving like other women her age, says Betsy, "Anything I did I did because I wanted to [….] Everyone I knew did it. Morals about that were supposed to be old-fashioned." [28]

Hector badgers and beats the faithful Betsy to force her to confess every detail of her past. While she is in Reno for six weeks, qualifying for a divorce to end the previous marriage that she considers meaningless, Hector writes that he has slept with someone else. He writes an explanation to Betsy of why his actions are justified: "It was on a purely carnal basis, good animal fun." Despite his fury over her past lovers, Hector sees this as a test for Betsy: "I feel clean, somehow. If you'll understand you'll be glad too. You'll be glad and you'll take it, as no one ever took it before." [29] Betsy hides her deep anguish at his infidelity, opting to act according to Hector's directive.

---

[27] Stansell 31-32
[28] *The Prodigal Women* 370
[29] Ibid. 391

Betsy succumbs to traditional expectations for behavior, evolving to a blandly satisfied earth mother. She gains strength from her relationship with Hector, although its torturous moments drag the reader down to the depths that led Hale to a nervous breakdown. The depiction is disappointing from the feminist perspective. Hale writes of Hector's feelings about Betsy's appearance. He rejects her modern career image in favor of a traditional conceptualization of woman: "There was something about long hair for a woman. They were hardly women without long hair. Women should be women; men should, they must, be men; and they could not be men until first the women were women." [30] Having built a strong and resourceful image of Betsy as a New York career woman, Hale strikes it down, burying her, along with her sister Maizie, in her desire to please a man. Hale writes of Betsy:

> "she had moulded herself upon the image he had held up before her, pushed before her, thrust before her; she had done it and done it, for months and months; beginning when she first met him. She had always been good at becoming things, she thought. The kind of women he wanted—the good woman, the faithful wife—she became." [31]

In the end, the only one of the three wanderers to arrive at any true sense of happiness is Betsy, who has molded herself into the image she feels that Hector desires. Betsy wants to be what he desires.

Hale develops a complex situation through Betsy and Hector, who endure as a couple despite his brutish methods of domination. They find a bond of strength through their need to be together. Betsy caves in to Hector's views, but both Nancy Hale and the character Maizie self-destruct when they trade

[30] Ibid. 478
[31] Ibid. 504

their individuality for partnership with domineering husbands. Hale leads the audience to question whether selfhood is, in itself, a social construct. Leda is the strongest of Hale's three prodigals; willfully in control of her own life, she finally chooses to relinquish parental rights to her own child. This conclusion is significant as a final battle in the emotional war of the novel. Like Leda, Hale shared equal custody of her own first child. During the writing of *The Prodigal Women*, she acknowledges in correspondence her anger at her son's preference for his father's family. Leda's decision to relinquish parental rights might be viewed as a self-conscious acquiescence to male authority or as a statement of female power. The final pages of the novel contain a lengthy self-analysis by Leda which is resolved at last by her acceptance of her difficulties with people. The stream-of-consciousness discussion, while lacking the control of Hale's description, is nonetheless noteworthy in its clear assertion of the protagonist as a being, relevant not by gender, but by individual spirit. On that assertion Hale stakes her claim as a writer and as a person.

Hale places a feminine slant on the parable of the prodigal son who destroys everything that he is given. Her women recklessly squander their youths on bad choices that dictate their futures. There is a feeling of resignation at last; their defiance burned out, all that remains are the ashes from the fire that guided them. Hale repeatedly challenges social constructs with boldness tempered by a modicum of acceptance of the ways of the past, placing her characters in positions of turmoil. In "The Bubble" a young woman leaves New York to spend the last two months of her pregnancy in Washington, D.C., in the large house of her mother-in-law. The story plants tradition alongside modern attitudes—treasured bonds of marriage and motherhood against the era's youthful hedonism. The narrator reflects on the events after many years have passed, and she draws the reader into the story quickly with her honesty; she is an eighteen-year-old woman in love with a man other than her husband. The impartial pronoun *it* refers to her unborn child. When labor begins, the trip to the hospital is particularly revealing of the clash in values: "I hadn't worn my wedding ring since I fell in love with Eugene. I'd told my mother-in-law that I didn't like the feeling of a ring, which was true. But in the taxi, in the darkness, she took off her own wedding ring and put it on my finger. 'Dear child,' she said, 'I just won't have you going to the hospital with no ring.' I remember I squeezed her hand." [32] In one instant Hale captures her own conflicted feelings about her progressive break with the social constructs in place at the time.

Hale won her first O. Henry Award with a 1933 story of pregnancy, significantly entitled "To the Invader." The story is told by a Northern woman visiting her husband's Virginia family during the first stage of her pregnancy. The narrator says, "You could have a baby in the North, and it was all shopping and talk and scrubbed clean shaven doctors, and in the end a neat hospital and a white nurse. Or you could, by strange and dreamy mischance, be pregnant in the South, and join an army of semi-tropic mothers, with gross arms and long hair, and become yourself a child-bearer. . . ." [33] The narrative opens with Angelica speculating about the future of her body: "She had her other hallucination now. She looked down at the straight narrow lines of her body lying under the heavy damp bedclothes. She was so little and flat that she only made a raised ribbon. But now she saw herself all bloated and huge, great with child, making an obscene hump in the middle of the bed with her stomach." [34] A review in the *New York Herald Tribune* summarizes the story as "a brief study of the hysteria of revolt rising in a slim Northern girl, pregnant and captive under the too solicitous and proprietary and hostile and so forth eyes of her Southern in-laws,

---

[32] "The Bubble" 21

[33] "To the Invader" 31

[34] Ibid. 31

whose women have always borne children, bulged and grown to bursting thereby." [35] When her mother-in-law seeks confirmation that the girl is "expectin'," she replies bluntly that she is indeed *pregnant*, at which "Mrs. Augustine coughed. That meant the word wasn't a nice one." [36] Both of these stories of pregnancy oppose the traditional Victorian image of the woman as caregiver, guarding the safety of a loving home. These women revile the distortion of their bodies by their condition and resent the loss of their sexual attractiveness. Hale's New Woman reflects the value system of the period that replaces wholesome simplicity with artificial refinement.

Hale repeatedly writes of the disparity in thinking between the generations. Social and moral differences are common between generations, but as twentieth century historian William E. Leuchtenburg points out about the years following World War I, "it may be doubted that there was ever a time in American history when youth had such a special sense of importance." He compares the divide to a fault in the earth. Young males had experienced the horrors of war, and "Young girls no longer consciously modeled themselves on their mother, whose experience seemed unusable in the 1920s." [37] He notes that the young lived lives of irresponsible hedonism.[38] Stanley Coben designates the 1920s as the first large scale rebellion against Victorian ideals, and he concludes that "The powerful assaults launched against Victorian culture during the twentieth century failed to replace most essential aspects of that culture with durable values, concepts, and institutions. . . ." [39] The modern movement offered freedom to experiment, but the people who experienced it had been raised to expect rules, and they spun helplessly, grabbing for something solid.

---

[35] NHP, SSC, 1.8

[36] "To the Invader" 33-34

[37] Leuchtenburg 173

[38] Ibid. 174

[39] Coben 35

Hale concludes *The Prodigal Women* with Leda's hostile attack on the traditional approach of Boston. Despite her own rejection of the rigid social decorum of Boston, she has just chosen to allow her son to be brought up exclusively in that world rather than continuing to share in his custody. She looks on the scene coldly:

> They were drinking their tea, smoking; invulnerable, untouched, untouchable. Armies could fling themselves against people such as these and when they fell back the people would be unscarred; unimpressed; drinking their tea.[40]

Hale pits North against South, male against female, and tradition against freedom. No one emerges unscathed, and by giving up her son to a traditional Boston upbringing, Leda appears to give up on her own version of the world.

Nancy Hale broke with the Victorian constructs of her mother's generation to write frankly about women as sexual beings with desires for satisfaction previously associated with males alone. She had described female adolescent stirrings of sexuality in stories like the popular "Midsummer," but in *The Prodigal Women* and again later in *The Sign of Jonah*, she tackles the desires of mature female protagonists. While Hale is overt in her descriptions which challenge traditional restrictions on women's behavior, she fails to endorse openly a feminist ideal. Her women possess individual desires—for one that is to be a career woman and for another it is to be the property of a man. It is difficult today to comprehend the impact that the narrative had on audiences in 1942. Nancy Hale's son was embarrassed when a boarding school master took his mother's book away from him because it was inappropriate reading. Today *The Prodigal Women* raises no eyebrows, but through it Nancy Hale revealed a fresh viewpoint. She exposed the requirements for

[40] *The Prodigal Women* 546

change of the era's women and the conflicts inherent in expressing those goals. Nancy Hale held feminist views, and she adopted the characteristic behaviors of feminists, but she never acted as a part of a movement. Hale felt that she acted as an individual, but she described behaviors which reflected the cultural constructs of her rebellious period in history.

Works Cited

Beebe, John. Personal Interview. 1 Feb. 2009.

Coben, Stanley. *Rebellion Against Victorianism: The Impetus for Cultural Change in 1920s America.* New York: Oxford UP, 1991.

Freeman, Anne Hobson. "Nancy Hale." *Dictionary of Literary Biography Yearbook:* 1980. Eds. Karen L. Rood, Jean W. Ross, and Richard Ziegfeld. Detroit: Gale, 1981. 212-219.

Friddell, Guy. "Spontaneous Book Product of Rewrites." *The Roanoke Times.* 18 May 1975. Clipping in SSC, NHP, 1.12.

Hale, Nancy. "The Bubble." *The New Yorker.* July 24, 1954, 20-24.

————. "Club Car." *The New Yorker.* Dec. 26, 1931, 42-43.

————. *The Prodigal Women.* New York: New American Library, 1988.

————. "To the Invader." *The Earliest Dreams.* New York: Scribner's, 1936. 30-42.

————. *The Young Die Good.* New York: Charles Scribner's Sons, 1932.

Leuchtenburg, William E. *The Perils of Prosperity, 1914-32.* Chicago: U of Chicago P, 1973.

Millett, Kate. *Sexual Politics.* 1968. Web.

Nancy Hale Papers. Sophia Smith Collection, Smith College, Northampton, MA.

The New Yorker, 26 August, 1933.

Perkins, Maxwell. *Editor to Author: The Letters of Maxwell E. Perkins.* Ed. John Hall Wheelock. New York: Scribner's, 1950.

Rowbotham, Sheila. *A Century of Women: The History of Women in Britain and the United States.* London: Viking, 1997.

Settle, Mary Lee. Introduction. *The Prodigal Women.* By Nancy Hale. New York: New American Library, 1988. vii-xiv.

Stansell, Christine. *American Moderns: Bohemian New York and the Creation of a New Century.* NewYork: Metropolitan Books, 2000.

Swinth, Kirsten. *Painting Professionals: Women Artists & the Development of Modern American Art, 1870-1930.* Chapel Hill: UNCP, 2001.

Essays on the Life of Nancy Hale

from *The Life in the Studio*

Eyes and No Eyes; or, the Art of Seeing

Nancy Hale

When my father got home from his Boston studio just before dinner at night, he would go at once to my mother's studio, on the north side of our house in Dedham, and see how her day's work had progressed.

"I need a crit!" she would cry, embracing him at the front door. The slang abbreviation, used by callow art students, carried certain nuances that, as a child growing up in that house, I was sensitive to. It suggested the relationship of master and pupil, and this in turn suggested an attitude of respect on my mother's part, which, while deeply sincere, was also a delicate and needed attention. My father, besides teaching anatomy and life drawing, was an art critic of note and phenomenally informed on art in general, but was not so successful a painter as my mother. When I was a child, she had more portrait orders than she could fill, and her prices were steadily rising. My father supported the household on his salary from the Boston Museum School; the money my mother earned was put carefully away in order to provide for an old age that, alas, since my father died at sixty-six, they never shared.

She was always successful, right from the start. My father told me with pride how, at the openings of exhibitions of even her earliest genre paintings and those charcoal drawings for which she had developed a sharpened-point technique wholly her own, one Boston dealer used to put up a velvet cord across the entrance until the cream of the buying cream had had a preliminary view. When the cord was taken down, every picture in the show would have been sold. Another dealer often used to say to her, "I can sell anything you do." By the time I was ten, my mother had become largely engaged in the painting of portraits. Certain intramural mysteries—the private jokes, the secret language of portrait painters—I picked up (in that village of commuting stockbrokers and bankers) the way a little Christian child in pagan Rome might have picked up the trick of how to draw fish in the sand with his toe.

My father would stand in the white-walled room—lamplit around half past six in the evening, or, if the season was summer, in the strong light of day—backing away from the canvas on the big easel and coming up close again to indicate with his thumb something he felt needed fixing. He was heavyset, with a walrus mustache that half concealed his mouth. He had a way of letting his hand drop to his side with a hard slap after making such an indication. Since he carried loose kitchen matches in his pocket to light his pipe with, at least once, in his life class, a student had timidly to say, "Mr. Hale, there's smoke coming out of your pocket."

My mother sat on her high painting stool, her chin propped on her fist, paying rapt attention; she looked like a Pre-Raphaelite damsel leaning out from the gold bar of Heaven; the room they were in was small and square. It had been just an ordinary room, until its whole north wall was replaced by windows, with short sash curtains that enabled my mother to make innumerable adjustments in the exact degree of that essential to painting as she knew it—the light.

On dark days she always called off a portrait sitting. She said she couldn't see anything when it was dark. Her eyes were certainly very different from lay eyes. When she and I went out shopping together, I could peer into the dark recesses behind a shopwindow and make out all sorts of objects—loaves of bread or garden rakes or magazines or whatever we might be looking for—while my mother, confronted by anything in deep shadow, would all her life simply say, "I can't see a thing."

One of her great artistic coups was inventing for herself a way of doing charcoal drawings of scenes in the falling snow—church spires, farmhouses, heavy-laden pines, which she indicated only as dark forms, leaving white paper for snow. These drawings were among the most sought-after examples of her work. On bitter, blizzardy winter mornings when my father and I would leave the house to walk to the village, a mile away, he to the train and I to school, he would remark, "Well, there's one comfort. She'll get something wonderful out of this."

When he was giving a criticism of one of my mother's portraits, he was likely to end up by saying, "Well! How do *they* like it?" Then they would laugh and make awful faces at each other.

But it was not always a laughing matter. Sometimes my mother was driven to despair by an objection a sitter, or a sitter's family, had made. "You know what Mr. G— said? 'I can't exactly say why, but somehow that just isn't my Margaret.'" She used the mocking tones in which, in our family, laymen were quoted.

"'A portrait's a picture with something the matter with the mouth'," my father would say, quoting Sargent.

Faced with real live laymen, my mother was very timid and anything but mocking. Sometimes this got her into trouble. A Mrs. W— had ordered a portrait of herself, and Mrs. W—'s

domineering old mother insisted that her daughter sit in a favorite pale-blue chiffon evening dress with a pale-blue feather
boa. "She looks so awful in it," my mother told my father.
"Like a glass of skim milk. I don't see it that way."

"Just tell them so," my father advised. "Tell them you can't
see it. You can't paint what you can't see."

My mother couldn't tell them so, however, and when the
portrait of the blond, blue-eyed Mrs. W— was finished, the
family did not like it. My mother withdrew the canvas and
painted another picture on its back, of our garden door, seen
from outside in full sunlight. The other day, when I was going
over old pictures, I came on Mrs. W—, looking at me after
thirty years. There she was, pale and wishy-washy, on the back
side of a painting of a brilliant green door, a scarlet trumpet
vine, and glimmering white china glimpsed within the interior.

My parents believed that a portrait should only be ordered
because the client wanted that particular artist's view. The
client presumably admired the artist's other work; in commis-
sioning a portrait, he was in effect paying to see himself, his
wife, or his children through those eyes. Yet clients were forever making their preposterous demands, not only about the
mouth or the dress but about how a sitter was to be posed
and what he was to be doing.

A rich, fashionable, and nice Mrs. B— ordered a portrait
of her four-year-old son. Children that young generally proved
difficult to keep still, but Mrs. B— took the time to come with
the boy herself and read to him during sittings. Reading aloud
was an essential in painting children, but was too often per-
formed by some nurse who read tonelessly, and bored the
child, which led to wriggling and squirming. Mrs. B—'s voice
was low, an excellent thing in woman; her choice of reading
matter just absorbing enough. The portrait of the fat little
tow-haired boy, wearing blue overalls and holding a red zinnia

he had snatched out of a vase the first morning, showed every promising sign for four or five sittings. Mrs. B— loving it. Then, one day, she brought her husband to see it.

"He hated it and he hated me," my mother reported to my father that night. "He slammed around this room, scowling and objecting to everything. What am I going to *do*?"

"Ignore him," my father advised.

"I can ignore his saying it doesn't look like his child. And I can endure his showing he didn't think it was any good," she said, though doubtfully. "But he says he won't have any son of his painted holding a flower."

"Oh, for God's sake!" my father said.

In the end, my mother took the flower out and painted the little boy with his hands clasped across his middle. Mr. B— accepted the portrait, though still scowling and objecting and refraining from one complimentary word. Years later, when I was grown up, I heard through friends of Mr. B—'s, who knew nothing of the history of the painting, that the old man, now a widower, loved the portrait of his son so dearly that he kept it in the Beacon Street library that was his favorite room, and moved it to his Nahant library every summer.

While people who paid for portraits by my mother might get their own way about what they wore in them, I, who had been since infancy the built-in, free artist's model around that house, never had any such say. My mother had drawn me at the age of six weeks in my bassinet; propped up against pillows, at the age of six months, on a background of patterned roses. At the age of one, seated in a baby carriage, I made a spot in an Impressionist painting by my father. There is a portrait of me at six wearing a dark-blue straw hat with red cherries, but that is the only article of apparel in a picture of me I remember having any fondness for, and even in that portrait I look glum. At seven I was posed with my hair parted in the middle and tied with two bows, too tight, which hurt. A prize-winning painting of my mother's called "Nancy and the Map of Europe" shows me and my large doll, dressed in identical blue cotton-crêpe dresses, with waistlines up under the armpits, and white guimpes. I hated dresses with high waist-lines, because the other girls wore dresses with low waistlines. For that matter, I hated my doll, too. I had to pose so much in my childhood that when I reached the age of about thirteen I finally figured out a requirement of my own. I wouldn't pose, I said, unless I could be painted with a book. So all subsequent pictures show me in the act of reading. Several are silhouetted against a window; some show the book, some don't; but all have the eyes downcast.

It was a day of knee-length skirts and hip-length waists, slave necklaces and cloche hats. My parents thought the fash-ions utterly hideous (I suppose they would think the same today.) They were right, of course. They seem always to have been right when it was a matter of how things looked. A Miss H— was painted by my mother as a débutante in a silver lace dress with a flame-colored rose on one hip. The dress ended just above the knee. My mother pled with the girl's mother to allow her to let the dress down or else cut the picture off above the edge of the dress—anything to avoid painting those two, separate knees. But the H—s were in the full swing of fashionable taste and brushed her pleas aside. They were de-lighted with the portrait when my mother finished it—knees and all. Years went by. So much later it seemed almost another life, my mother ran into an aged, sweet-faced Mrs. H— at a tea. She pressed my mother's hand in hers and said, "I have a little idea! Would you—could you—touch up Carolyn's por-trait? I don't know if it is possible to add a little something, just to cover the knees? I wonder if you can visualize what I mean...."

"Can I visualize what she means!" my mother snorted to me. My father was dead by that time. "*Can* I visualize!"

She did paint in some silver lace over those knees, which had, Mrs. H— confessed, caused the picture to be relegated to the attic. It had to be a piece of real silver lace, though. Mrs. H— had to find such a piece, and it had to be tacked onto a silvery-gray dress for a live model to wear. My mother and father had the utmost contempt for painters who painted things out of their heads. Not that they wanted to paint what is sometimes called photographically; far from it. They wanted to "render the object"—an immensely subtle process involving the interplay of the painter's subjective view with the way the light actually fell upon the object. The conflict—rather, the marriage—of objectivity and subjectivity was what made art such a wildly exciting and magical thing to my parents that they cared about literally nothing else, except maybe me. To have made up a piece of silver lace out of her head would, in my mother's view, have been unintelligent, boring, and by her standards ultimately impossible. How could she possibly know, unless she saw, just how the light would make it look?

As an art student for some fifteen years in Paris, my father spent a good deal of time at Giverny, close to Monet, and was influenced by Impressionist theories. What seemed important to him and, through him, to my mother about Monet's haystacks, cathedrals, and water lilies was that, painted at a different time of day and hence in a different light, each picture was in effect of a totally different subject from the others in the same series. Objects existed as seen in the light of the moment. Half an hour later, in another light, they became quite other objects.

In his class in life drawing at the Museum School, moreover, my father taught his students to render the nude in strict light and shade. Some pupils seemed never to be able to learn to find the edge of the shadow, on one side of which all was visible and to be shown, on the other side of which all was considered invisible. I took that class, when I was eighteen. I can see my father now, standing under the stark atelier skylight in his rumpled old gray suit, backing up from some student's smudgy charcoal drawing and coming up to it again, making gestures with his thumb (he never touched a pupil's drawing) and wearing a pained expression.

"Where the light falls is the light. Where the light does *not* fall is the shadow. Chiaroscuro, the clear and the obscure. Don't go mucking your drawing up with half-lights." Half-lights were the snare that seduced the under-trained; the greatest sin was to go peering into the shadow.

When my mother looked at things (and her life was given over to looking at things; in any unfamiliar house she used to keep crying "Look at that! Look at that!" about a chair, a picture, a china bowl of flowers, until she became embarrassed by the realization that nobody else joined her), she looked with a kind of innocent, once-born stare. I can see that now, too. She held her eyes very wide open and simply stared, as though confronted by the first day of creation.

Often she saw things quite differently from other people. Colors, for instance, appeared different to her from what they seemed to me to be. She would keep talking about a blue house on the road to Gloucester, and I couldn't imagine what she was talking about, and then one day we would be driving that road together and she would cry, "There's the blue house! Look at that!" I would look, and it would be white.

"You're so *literary*," my father and mother used to complain to me. This was in no sense a compliment but referred to the instantaneous reflex of reading into color what I figured it had to be, instead of seeing it for what—in that light—it was. I remember a dress my mother owned in the latter part of her life. She called it her black dress. Although it was a very dark dress, I couldn't help knowing that it was really navy blue. It did take peering to see that, though, and my mother never peered. She just stared, and her vision and the image met for what they were.

Then there was the portrait my mother painted of Miss R——, another Boston débutante of the late twenties, whom she posed sitting sidewise, leaning forward, arms resting on a table, head turned so that it was seen three-quarters. For once, my mother plucked up the courage to assert what the sitter was to wear. Miss R—— and her mother wanted the dress in which Miss R—— had made her début. I don't think I ever saw it, but I can imagine it—hip-girdled, knee-exposing, "snappy," as we used to say. But my mother had her way, and painted Miss R—— in a Chinese robe that a missionary in-law of ours brought back from China, of dark-blue, stiff, gauzy material encrusted with gold-embroidered dragons. Only, in the painting, it was green with silver.

The R——s viewed the finished painting with pronounced disfavor. Not only was a mere three-quarters of their daughter's face visible (and, they may have reasoned, they were paying for the whole face) but she was wearing a garment that didn't remotely resemble any clothes they admired, or, for that matter, the actual Chinese robe, either—a robe demonstrably dark blue, not green. They let it be known, politely, that they could not accept the portrait.

My mother never minded when a portrait came back on her hands, because, flooded with orders as she was in those days, she always needed something to send to the exhibitions, all over the country, to which her work was invited. Portraits in private hands were hard to borrow, for people hate lending portraits; it is as if one asked for the fireplace out of their living room.

Somewhere beyond our ken Miss R— grew older, got married, had children, lost her husband, began acquiring grandchildren, and then, out of the blue, years later, when my mother had come to Virginia to live near me, came a letter from Miss R— to ask whether, if the portrait was still in existence, she might see it with a view to buying it. She did see it, and bought it with enthusiasm.

It was not only the clothing of women my mother found unpaintable. Male clothing was even worse. "That awful V," she called the effect a man's collar and tie make, and she invented a way to circumvent having to paint it by getting men sitters to wear scarves. (Men sitters seem to have been more amenable than women, perhaps because the artist was so beautiful.) I can remember only one portrait of hers of a man not wearing a scarf—that of the Reverend Dr. Lyman Rutledge, whom she painted in his academic robes, which came up high enough partly to obscure "that awful V."

Little boys, back in the days of Miss R—'s youth, presented no problem, since, for best, they wore light-colored linen suits with lace or linen collars and, for every day, shorts, that showed their bare legs. By my mother's latter days, however, even the smallest boys had taken to dressing like "dreadful little men," in dark suits with shirts, ties, and long pants—"two long black tubes" she called them.

My mother's apartment in Virginia was small, what is locally called a duplex—half of a one-story house. She had chosen it entirely because the principal room had a view window that went up to the ceiling and let in enough light to make it suitable for a studio. She had an ingrained prejudice against the custom of keeping window shades at half mast. Any window shade over which she had any control was instantly raised to the top. What other people call the glare she called the light.

In the South, she discovered, people were not accustomed to thinking in terms of her rather high prices for portraits. If she wanted to go on getting portrait orders, she would have to lower them. She did want to go on getting them. She never even considered the contrary. Nothing irritated her more when she was an old lady than to have someone say, "Do you still paint?" She reduced her prices to less than a third of her Northern high. Even so, there were difficulties. The wife of a multi-millionaire Detroiter who had retired to Albemarle County came up to me one day in the grocery store and, after beating about the bush, said she had seen some of my mother's portrait drawings and would love to have her grand-sons done. How much, she ventured with hesitation to ask, did my mother charge? I told her. (It was now less than two hundred dollars for a drawing.) "Oh," cried the Detroit lady, in her mink coat. "Oh! I'm afraid I couldn't possibly afford that!" And she hurried away to the meat counter.

The Southern ladies, too, experienced great mortification in bringing themselves to speak of money to so beautiful and elegant a person as my mother. They came to me to ask her portrait prices in a sort of agony. "I just *couldn't* ask her how much she charges," said the mother of two sons who were later done by my mother with vast success. "She's such a *lady.*"

My mother felt no such qualms. "Good heavens! Does she think I do it for nothing?" she'd say. "You'd think I was some damned amateur."

My mother never swore, normally; but to my father amateurs were always "damned amateurs," and my father's locu-tions lived on in my mother's vocabulary. His principles, too, remained forever hers. Once when some sitter's hard-luck story had tempted her to present him with his portrait (it is amazing the impoverishment people who think nothing of new Buicks feel when it comes to portraits), she ended by stiffening and saying, "No. Your father used to say, 'Never give away your work. People don't value what they don't have to pay for.'"

The portraits she did in Virginia were much admired, and contented clients went out of their way to bring prospective sitters to her. One such client telephoned to ask if she might bring a Mrs. W— to tea on Thursday to see examples of my mother's work. My mother spent the intervening days hanging additional pictures, which had been out in her little storeroom, on the walls. When four o'clock Thursday came, the two women arrived. They drank tea, chattered volubly, stayed for an hour or so, and then made their departure. At the door my mother's client said, "I'm so sorry you weren't able to find some pictures for us to look at."

"I was so stunned I couldn't think of one word to say," my mother told me next day. "I just stood there gaping, with this whole place plastered with my work in back of me. What did they think I was going to do—push them in their faces?"

She could never get used to the idea that most people don't use their eyes except to keep from running into things. She never learned not to feel wounded when, for example, she'd made some charming arrangements of flowers for the table, or placed a yellow chair in a telling position against a rose toile curtain, and not one person at the party for which the effect had been planned made any comment. "Nobody liked it!" she'd wail. I had to keep persuading her that other people didn't see what she saw. "You mean they didn't see it? But it was right in front of them," she'd cry with an incredulity undiminished over the years.

I and my friends were really hardly any better, being writers and fairly sightless too. Once, at our seashore place in Massachusetts, after a number of literary people had passed through for a longer or shorter time, all with eyes downcast to the glacial boulders underfoot or the murmurous water below, while they talked and talked of their own and other writers' work, my mother exploded.

"Here they've come to what is *probably* the most beautiful view on the Eastern Seaboard," she said, and they don't look at one thing! They might just as well stay in New York."

If art as she understood it alienated her from the sightless all her life, during her last years it alienated her from modern painters as well. They, too, gazed at the ground, painted by electric light, peered into the shadow—all of which was against her artistic religion. Years before, my father had been fond of declaring that modernists—meaning painters since Cezanne—were in effect saying, "Let me look into the interior of my belly."

That attitude in modern painting was what profoundly distressed her. It was not at all that modern pictures were abstractions. "Every good painting is basically an abstraction," my father used to say. Or that they were not representational. Her dismay was different from the layman's dismay. What depressed her was the loss of that rapturous meeting between the artist's private vision and the shimmering world of objects. To her it amounted to a loss of soul.

Although there always remained a demand for my mother's portraits—"When a woman wants a portrait of her children, she wants it to look like them," she would comment grimly—her work went out of style within her own lifetime. No longer was she invited to show at all the big exhibitions over the country. She did still show at some, and she did still win an occasional prize; but she, who had once sold every picture out of her exhibitions before they officially opened, now experienced that pendulum swing of fashion which, in the art of painting, is perhaps more extreme than in any other.

She had only contempt for painters of her own generation who, cannily trimming their sails to the prevailing winds, turned out Abstract Expressionism. She couldn't believe they were being honest. She couldn't believe that anyone who had ever got into intimate artistic relation with the natural world could be satisfied by communion with self alone. Half of reality had been abandoned, it seemed to her; the inner half remained, alone and impotent. If it was against her religion to go peering into the shadow, it was even more against it to avert the eyes from that world upon which the light falls.

The year my mother died, at eighty-three, we went to Italy to see the pictures. She had seen the British and French paintings years before, but never the Italian. Among exclaiming sightseers looking up at the blackened Tintorettos that line the dim walls and ceilings of the Scuola San Rocco, in Venice, my mother merely stared at the pictures for a bit and said, "I can't see anything at all."

"But look!" the friend traveling with us cried. "Just look—hard—at the wonderful drapery in that one above!"

"I can't see a thing," my mother repeated. Where the light fell was the light. Where the light did not fall was the shadow. Chiaroscuro—the clear and the obscure.

She loved looking at such paintings as had been provided with spotlights, in various galleries and churches, and she loved looking at everything in the Uffizi, where the light falls white and strong. Most of everything in Italy she loved the radiant Tuscan landscape. As she stared at the undulating olive groves we drove through, the walled towns, the castle-topped hills, I could see by her engrossed look that the special marriage of subject and object was occurring for her.

We sailed home from Genoa on an American liner. It was making the last leg of a Mediterranean cruise, and we shared a table with a retired admiral and his wife—affable people of the world. My mother and the admiral's wife, who was called something like Mrs. Haughton, seemed made to get on with each other, as two antique, elegant, and still beautiful women. Mrs. Haughton plied my mother with questions—about her genealogy, receiving answers most gratifying to her; about the problem of becoming dress for the elderly; about mutual acquaintances, of which they discovered several. Most of these were ex-sitters of my mother's—a relationship Mrs. Haughton found it slightly difficult to grasp. "Oh, you're artistic!" she finally exclaimed, her face clearing. My mother winced.

One day the Haughtons turned up for lunch, full of a party they had just been to in the captain's quarters. It had been a cocoa party, they reported, making a good story of it. The captain, it appeared, was a teetotaler. At noon Mrs. Haughton, as the oldest lady present, had been given the honor of pulling the cord that blew the ship's whistle. You could see what a kick the pretty old lady got out of it. "When you heard that great WHOOOO, that was me!" she said.

I took it for granted the Haughtons rated their invitation to the bridge as old Navy people. But next day we, too, found an engraved card slipped under our stateroom door inviting us to the captain's quarters at half after eleven. The captain turned out to be a handsome man of some sixty years, who told me that in his seafaring youth he had been so terrified by a tidal wave off Maderia that he never touched liquor again. The guests were handed cards printed with a recipe for the cocoa we were drinking, which was excellent. As noon approached, the captain asked my mother, delicately, if she thought perhaps she was the senior lady present.

"Yes indeed; I'm a great-grandmother," she replied.

"That beats all the grandmothers here!" the captain declared and invited her to blow the ship's whistle at twelve.

The time came, and we all—some eight or ten of us—

trooped out onto a little deck off the chartroom, where a sharp breeze was blowing. In the brilliant sunshine the ocean all around us was ruffled into peaks.

The moment came; my mother pulled the cord; and the great, deep, thrilling whistle sounded. Then we went inside. Everyone congratulated my mother on being the oldest lady present, on being a great-grandmother, on blowing the whistle.

At lunch the admiral's lady leaned across the table, her eyes sparkling. "I hear it was you who blew the whistle today!" she said. "*How* exciting!"

After lunch, when we had gone to our stateroom for a nap, my mother said, "What's so wonderful about blowing a whistle? Here I've given my whole life to painting and nobody on board says one single word about my work. All they notice is that I'm the oldest woman alive, for pity's sake."

I started to tell her no one on board would ever have heard of her work; but I couldn't.

"Did you see, though," my mother continued, "the way the ocean looked, when we went out, with the sun on it? Bright, transparent green."

"I'd call it blue," I had to say.

"You would," she said. Affectionately.

1965

Nancy Hale and
the Art of Memoir

G. Thomas Tanselle

⊶⊷

I first encountered Nancy Hale in the pages of *The New Yorker* in the 1950s. She had been publishing short stories there since the early 1930s—with such regularity that she was one of the three or four people who symbolized the magazine for me during my earliest steady reading of it. Although I admired her stories, the piece that struck me most forcefully, and made a lasting impression on me, was not fiction but memoir: "What Haunts Thee in Fond Shapes," which appeared in the issue of 5 August 1967—that title being one of several allusions to the Bhagavad Gita in her writings. In this essay Hale describes the process of clearing out her mother's studio after her mother—the celebrated painter Lilian Westcott Hale—had died. As she examines object after object, she explores in many cases the associations each item has for her—the bits of her mother's life, as known to her, and of her own, that it captures. Even when she only names the objects, the succession of details is in itself evocative.

That physical objects are rich with associations was not an idea new to me when I read this piece in 1967. I had been a purposeful book collector for over ten years, and I was well aware of how many stories are encapsulated in the traces left in books by their former owners. I had also begun work as a bibliographical scholar—that is, one who studies books as objects, in order to follow the clues they provide to book-production history and, in turn, to the history and authority of textual variations. In other words, I was dealing with the human associations of physical objects, for I was paying attention to what particular typesetters and designers had done at specific past moments. Hale's 1967 essay came to me at exactly the right time: I was prepared to ponder the ideas that underlay it and to allow them to enrich my own thinking.

After the first few lines of the piece, Hale embarks on a long catalogue of objects, which immediately enchanted me, and does so still whenever I reread it:

> the half-empty pots of glue and linseed oil and turpentine; the balsa-wood plane models, broken, my son made while my mother was painting him; coils of wire used on boats for some purpose; cigar-boxes of dried-up paint tubes; the conch shells in the still-life composition that was the last thing my mother painted before she died; the rotted leather trunks full of photographs mounted on cards in the Victorian manner, of ladies in bustles, gentlemen with beards, once somebody's friends but now forever unknown; a yellow luster vase; a pair of desiccated rubber gloves for handling the etching plates in an acid bath; a pile of old *Transactions* of the Brontë Society; several palettes, still set, the blobs of paint dried as hard as multicolored marbles; plaster casts, damaged, of Aphrodite, of a della Robbia *bambino*, of an *écorché*—a model of the nude stripped to show the muscles; a pile of old pochades my father painted on one of his infrequent visits away from his Boston studio, of apple blossoms against the sea; several cheap camp-stools for outdoor painting, and several sketching easels, but no two of them in the same place . . . .

I have quoted less than half of the full list, but enough to illustrate the artistry of the whole, though the incantatory effect is increased when one reads all of it. What appear to be random objects that successively catch Hale's attention are in fact an artfully constructed series. First is a group of fairly expected items (glue, oil, turpentine), followed by something unexpected (plane models); the first relates primarily to her mother, the second connects her and her son with her mother, since the planes entertained the son while his portrait was being painted. The poetry of the ordinary is enriched by the specificity of the adjectives ("half-empty," "balsa-wood") and the rhythms created by the repeated "and" ("glue and linseed oil and turpentine") and the insertion of "broken" between commas ("models, broken, my son made"). These techniques continue through the entire list, which actually conveys a considerable amount of information, such as (in the part quoted) the fact that her father was also a painter. Catalogues have an ancient literary heritage; and, as here, they often exhibit pleasure in similes ("as hard as multicolored marbles"), in startling juxtapositions (a luster vase and rubber gloves), and in the sheer sounds of the names for things ("conch shells," "bustles," "pochades") and of proper nouns ("Brontë," "Aphrodite," "della Robbia"). Furthermore, the elegiac air lambently hovering over it all is enhanced by occasional extraneous observations—such as, after the reference to photographs of Victorian ladies and gentlemen, the addition of these words: "once somebody's friends but now forever unknown."

Having plunged the reader at once into the ambience of the studio with this bravura performance (which could stand on its own as a poem), Hale turns to still other objects in a more leisurely manner, thinking about them in answer to various forms of the question "What am I to do with ——?" Some call up extended ruminations, including an account of the construction in 1911 of the granite cottage at Folly Cove in Rockport, Massachusetts, housing "this studio by the sea," given to her mother by her aunt in 1931. (She does not name names, except for that of her grandfather, Edward Everett Hale; but her father, Philip Leslie Hale, and his sister, Ellen Day Hale, as well as her mother, were prominent in the Boston art scene of their time.) Several people had advised her to discard everything ("junk," as her husband called it), but the thought of throwing it all out makes her "quail": "Even to imagine beginning to is like opening, in a dream, a nightmare closet upon confusion. I feel I can't." As she lingers over these items, she repeatedly recognizes that they speak of "a real time, a real place"; that they are "keys to release the life that trembles behind them in the void"; that they "seem worlds in themselves." After her reverie, she is brought back to the present by "the noise the flies of noonday make," and she prepares to join her friends who are swimming in the cove: "*Love calls us to the things of this world*, I repeat to myself as I go to change into my suit. True, but then what do you call what I feel for all this junk, these worlds?" There is no better evocation of the process of going through the possessions of a person who has died—and, more generally, of the power of objects to conjure up the past and serve as a focus for assessing it.

Two years after Hale published this sketch, she used it as the opening chapter of *The Life in the Studio*—the title referring not simply to the past, but to the life brought into the studio in the present by the objects that remain. The book collects fifteen pieces, mostly from *The New Yorker*, which are gathered under two headings, the first eight under "Family Ties" and the other seven under "Loosenings," reflecting the progression the book subtly depicts. (The second half begins, like the first, with the stone house, where the smell of oil paint and turpentine remains.) Although there is no subtitle on the title page, the dust-jacket supplies an accurate one: "An Affectionate Recollection of Some Singular Parents." Besides shrewd, complex characterizations of her parents, however, there are also revealing glimpses (some extensive) of her aunt Ellen and

Ellen's companion, her grandparents on both the Hale and Westcott sides (and other members of their generation), and childhood neighbors. A picture emerges of life in a still rural suburb of Boston (Dedham) in the 1910s and 1920s, interrupted with scenes of whatever places her linked memories take her—the Rockport stone house, of course, but also the older cottage down the hill from it, her father's Boston studio, the Westcott place in Westchester County, a *pensione* in Venice, two residences in Charlottesville. The present and what she now imagines the past to have been are rendered through the novelist's mixture of poetic exposition and invented conversation. Suffusing the book is a joyous relishing of life; but the pleasure is alloyed with the knowledge of disappointment, suffering, illness, and death and an awareness of poverty, social injustice, deceit, and war. One source of childhood happiness came from realizing, "Other families . . . did not seem to have the same attachment to each other that we had." Yet her childhood was "overlaid by a haze of melancholy." The mixture of joy and sadness is epitomized by her beautifully detailed account of the exuberance she felt as a child on the day after the school year ended: "I was bursting with my freedom," she writes, as "summer was just beginning to glisten and to sing." But suddenly—into her "state of heaven there crawled like a maggot" the recollection of the day when she noticed and reported that a neighbor's horse, riderless, had come down the same path where she was now walking: the neighbor had fallen from the horse and became a permanent invalid.

Although much of the book does not deal explicitly with "the life in the studio," the opening sketch reverberates throughout—not only in the continual echoing of the phrase "the stone house by the sea" and its variations, but also in references to clearing out other accumulations. The life that resides in physical things is central to most of the joined recollections. When, for instance, Hale puts away after-dinner coffee cups in her Virginia house, she remembers that they—

with their "little bunches of Dresden flowers"—were in the dining-room china cabinet of her childhood house in Dedham; this thought takes her to a vase now in the living room, from the same cabinet, that gives her "a feeling carried over, like freight"; she is then led to her mother's opinions on china-painting. The "little white enamel teapot"—which, she says, "I used today for my breakfast coffee"—figures as the receptacle for hot paraffin in an extended account of her mother's jelly-making during World War I. Even the gardens around the stone house, as she tries to keep them under control, are reminders of what her mother chose to plant at each spot, and then of her parents' winter reading of seed catalogues for their Dedham garden. In the final chapter, "An Arrangement in Parents" (continuing in its title the motif of painters' terminology), she describes her elation one day walking up Lexington Avenue, remembering simultaneously that her father had told her of the same experience. "It gave a sort of solidity to my euphoria that my father had felt it before me, and it was one of the ways in which my parents began to rearrange themselves." Although this particular "rearrangement" arose from her physical surroundings as a whole, not a specific object, it was the same shift in perception that every object with associations can produce. The mingling of past and present, when meditated upon, generates new insights into both. *The Life in the Studio* is a glorious book, and it deserves to be regarded as a classic of the memoir genre.

G. Thomas Tanselle, former vice president of the John Simon Guggenheim Memorial Foundation, teaches at Columbia University and serves as president of the Bibliographical Society of the University of Virginia and co-editor of the Northwestern-Newberry Edition of the writings of Herman Melville. He has previously served as president of the Bibliographical Society of America, the Grolier Club, and the Society for Textual Scholarship.

With Artists as Parents:
on *The Life in the Studio*

John Beebe

———— ∞ ————

I first read *The Life in the Studio* as a Hale family friend. I had known not only the author herself, but two of the close relatives that she describes in the book: her son Bill, my fellow student at Harvard, and her mother, Lilian Wescott Hale, who made two charcoal drawings of me when I turned eighteen and a third when I was twenty-one. The summer of 1957, when I first posed for her, I was staying with all of them in the stone house, Howlets, at Folly Cove that embodied for Nancy Hale the enduring pleasures of the artist's life. That life, I realized from the first days of my first visit, had become the family's shared fate, and it impressed me too as the perfect way to live. I knew of course that such perfection came at something of a cost, though what precisely that was did not become clear to me until I read Nancy's book. Then I thought that the toll was living under the shadow—and with the ghosts

—of people one has long thought more creative and accomplished than oneself. Now, after reading the book again, over forty years later, I realize that even more is exacted of those who propose to create out of what they have actually seen and experienced, which is the kind of artist both Nancy and Lilian were: one has to be willing to accept the work of mourning all the lost life one has only partly succeeded in getting down on paper or canvas. That Nancy succeeds in doing this work of mourning in *The Life in the Studio* makes her memoir a psychological masterpiece, one that illumines not just the artist's life as she understands it, but also our common need to recreate the lives of those who have made a difference to us. Her accomplishment gives me heart to attempt to recover for a present-day audience the more general insights that her grief-work led her to, and to reflect on how it shapes the genre of autobiography that we encounter when we read her book, a genre both old and new, the signal virtues of which make us wonder how we could have lost sight of this way of reflecting on the past.

One of this genre's virtues is a trust in memory. There is a telling exchange between Nancy and her son Bill, then still at Harvard, when she offends him by singing "Buck the line for Harvard, For Harvard wins today..." He corrects her, drily, that "the actual words are 'Hit the line for Harvard,'" adding "in case you are interested," but she effectively counters his dismay at the liberty she felt she could take with the rallying song of his superordinate alma mater with "I know, but I'm singing Grandpa's words." [1] The memory she stands up for signals the complicated psychological relationship Nancy's father, Philip Hale, held with Harvard, which she proceeds to explore. Alone of the men in his immediate family, her father did not attend Harvard, though he could easily have

---

[1] *The Life in the Studio* 64

gotten into what had become his family's school. "Bucking" the line for Harvard is, to put it crudely, what he ended up doing: inadvertently buttressing the Establishment view of what was appropriate by taking an independent path of training as an artist and not a teacher and critic of art—activities in which he eventually turned out to excel, and for which a Harvard degree might have qualified him to teach at a university rather than the School of the Museum of Fine Arts in Boston. Nancy does not know enough to draw that conclusion more than intuitively for the reader: all she has to go on is the way her father chose to sing the words to the Harvard fight song, reserved for the Harvard-Yale game, and the fact that she associates his singing it with attending such a game with her uncle, who had gone to Harvard, and watching her father come back to the stands, thinking himself out of Nancy's earshot, say: "You take just one bum steer and your whole damned life seems to go down the drain." She recalls, "A trickle of terror chilled me, and under my feet the abyss yawned. My father *not* happy?" [2] And then, without further explanation, the game is on, Harvard wins, and her father starts singing the fighting song with words of his own invention before ending with the commonly-recognized finale: "for Harvard wins today." Nancy Hale lets her readers draw their own conclusion as to the meaning of her father's having laid down, and her artist's voice to have followed, this alternative route to an unchanged ending; so I can only say that, for me, her father's way of rendering it reveals that the establishment notion of the path to success, a Harvard education, from which he had consciously chosen to deviate in his passion to become an artist, had managed nevertheless to prevail in his unconscious, and would ever, in his mature years, cast a melancholy shadow over the way he perceived his destiny.

[2] Ibid. 70

Here, as in other places, *The Life in the Studio* precisely calculates the social costs of choosing to be an artist. This too has become a nearly forgotten subject, because the Establishment, since the mid-1960s, when much of this book was written, has lost its purchase on the imagination. Today, fall from the grace of respectability often secures, for artists, respect for the individual path. It becomes a sign that they have paid their dues. Present-day biographies, especially when they are written by Americans, celebrate Oscar Wilde and Arthur Rimbaud as heroic pioneers, not (as in the literary circles Nancy's son and I were part of when we were undergraduates majoring in English) warning signals that too much individuality in one's acculturation can spell ruin for oneself and others.

No such retrospective rescue from the insecurity of being an artist is granted to the painters Nancy remembers in this book. One of its themes is how far the practice of art can be pursued in the studio without accompanying attrition, at other levels of the human building, to those rooms most people who are not artists inhabit and in which they grow and develop. One of the most exquisite chapters begins the book's second section called, a bit ambiguously, "The Loosening," which seems to me to refer to the lysis of the "sophisticated" judgments she formed in her early twenties, after she had moved to New York and begun to work for *Vogue*, as to the unworldliness of her immediate New England impressionist forbears pursuing their version of the creative life. "Joyous Gard" (the title of the chapter comes from the Arthurian stories that Nancy loved, where it is the name given Sir Lancelot's destined castle after he has broken the spell that had formerly made it "dolorous") is about the stone studio by the sea, and its first owner, Nancy's aunt, Ellen Day Hale, who before Nancy's father had studied painting in Paris in the 1880s and had built it as a place to do printmaking. In Nancy's initially disapproving view, Aunt Nelly was an "old maid," though she maintained a Boston marriage of sorts with her much more extroverted friend Gabrielle de Veaux Clements, another American Impressionist, and as Nancy enviously recalls, had "a wonderful time" living the artist's life unencumbered by patriarchal marriage. The sacrifice required, in Aunt Nelly's case, went even further. Nancy ventures her own surety that Ellen Day Hale was never sexual, and ends the chapter with this evocation of her intuition, watching Nelly as she was dying, that her aunt's life had belonged, at heart, to an eternal child, or even to a child unborn, as if that were the condition attached to the privilege of being eternally devoted to what has yet to be created:

> As she lay on her side in bed, increasingly her emaciated, battered old knees were being drawn toward her bony chest until, the last time I saw her, she was totally and irrevocably curled up, as though grotesquely illustrating, in that antique frame, the child born of a virgin she had painted on canvas so often. It was hardly an apotheosis of her life, much less a promise of richer life to come, but a sort of literal exposition of life's core.[3]

The heart of the book is Nancy's lifelong struggle to understand her mother. The Jungian analyst Joseph Wheelwright, who grew up around Boston and had dated Nancy Hale when he was 14 and she 15, had known Nancy's father (whom he regarded as a "bounder" for the womanizing that Nancy finally faces with exquisite taste in these pages), and after he and I had both read *The Life in the Studio*, he summarized its deep process for me by saying that "she worked through her father and found her mother." In the late 1960s, Jo had an office in the same building in San Francisco as my own Jungian analyst, whom I was seeing en route to training in the very Institute Jo had helped to found. He would come out and chat with me

---

[3] Ibid. 114

when I was waiting for my analyst to arrive to take me into his office for our "hour." I had told Jo that I had written to Nancy that the way she deals with her parents, in the course of mourning them in *The Life in the Studio*, was "the most passionate description of working-through" that I had ever read. This was not necessarily surprising, given Nancy's own enduring commitment to the analysis she had undergone, after suffering a major depression in the 1940s, with Beatrice Hinkle, one of the very first Jungian analysts on the East Coast, who established a sanitarium in a mansion in Washington, CT where she could offer inpatient service to people who needed more containment than her outpatient practice could provide.[4]

What I find interesting about *The Life in the Studio* is not that it consists of the kind of symbolic ruminations on personal matters that one might expect in the wake of a Jungian analysis, but rather that it shows their continuing necessity in the shaping of her own creative life. According to Nancy, who often referred to it in the course of our friendship, her treatment with Dr. Hinkle was a success. It was undertaken in the 1940s, in the aftermath of a frightening bout of writer's block that had threatened to paralyze her literary career, and it re-established her creative initiative to such a degree that she was able to establish a record by selling twelve stories to *The New Yorker* in a single year. The past exacted its own price, however, in the degree to which Nancy's subsequent individuation as an artist seems to have depended on getting her parents' story right. She had actually prepared her readers for a book that would make this aim central with the final paragraph of her Introduction to *A New England Girlhood*, the book she published in 1958, sixty-five years after the same publisher, Little Brown, had published her grandfather, Edward Everett Hale's *A New England Boyhood*:

------

[4] Hale creates a similar setting for her novel *Heaven and Hardpan Farm*, published in 1957, four years after Dr. Hinkle's death.

My pieces, although their background is the scenery and characters that bounded my childhood, are intended less to be about the real and ascertainable past than about my memory of it; and memory, as a mode of thinking, tends to burst spontaneously into fantasy at every turn. Some of the events in the stories are true to fact, some not. What interested me in writing them was to try to catch the reverberations from childhood that sometimes make it seem as if the first few years of all our lives constitute a riddle which it is a lifework to solve.[5]

One reason Nancy may have had to work at solving this puzzle well into the years that many of us feel like moving beyond the problem of parents, is that her parents' project was in a sense incomplete, and that she, as their only child, not only inherited it (with no siblings to share it with), but was, as a similar kind of artist, charged with making sense of it. Their project, in artistic terms, was realizing impressionism on American soil. For them, as native New Englanders, this was a soil that had been enriched by Emersonian perfectionism, and they saw it as their duty to till it in a way that would make their form of art survive. Edward Everett Hale, Philip Hale's father (whom Lilian had also accepted as her *spiritus rector*), had been close to Emerson and on the occasion of the ninetieth anniversary of the philosopher's birth, May 25, 1893, Dr. Hale managed to articulate the standard that had been set by his friend:

He was a man of ideals, but not a dreamer, and he taught men how to live a true life because he lived one himself. His mission was to elevate truth and honor, and he did not waste time in attempting to vilify falsehood and sham.... Emerson's sturdy common sense saved him from his host of imitators.[6]

---

[5] Hale 1958, p xvi

[6] "In Eulogy of Emerson"

It was this standard that the Hales, both of whom won Gold Medals at International Expositions—Philip in 1910, Lilian in 1915—had set for themselves as artists. When I met her, Mrs. Hale was still living it. When she drew me, she stood absolutely erect and could be withering when I, prematurely weary of posing, would slouch. She never tired: her arm moved almost like a lever, up and down, so as to bring her hand back and forth over the impressive wooden easel, a movement that allowed her to choose when the charcoal in her hand would touch the paper. Working within an ever-hovering commitment to the integrity of what she was drawing, she made sure it never did unless its mark would fall where it should. On the fine parchment, my eighteen-year-old image— a youth still mostly lost in his own dreams, but nevertheless moved to notice what most stood out around him (in this case, the astonishing diligence of the gorgeous white-haired 76-year-old artist in her maroon cardigan sweater and black skirt)—came into view, spirited into a permanence I would not have risked myself to attain.

In the second chapter of *The Life in the Studio*, "Eyes and No Eyes. Or the Art of Seeing," Nancy Hale gives a similar permanence to her father's doctrine of impressionism. She recalls him telling his class, which she had taken at the same age I was when first posing for her mother, "Where the light falls is the light. Where the light does *not* fall is the shadow. Chiaroscuro, the clear and the obscure. Don't go mucking your drawing up with half-lights." [7] One of the outstanding characteristics of this memoir is the way Nancy distinguishes what was clear about her parents, because also clear *to* them— the philosophy of art by which they lived—from the psychological shadows they could not see, and which Nancy was destined to feel, to suffer, and finally to understand. That was

[7] *The Life in the Studio* 21

her legacy, and, as a writer blessed with what Keats called "negative capability," she proves herself able to redeem the shadow of her parents' marriage, the fly in the ointment of their lives, precisely by recognizing its obscurity for them. Here is the way she sets up, for the reader, the inevitability of that shadow coming to threaten *them* with obscurity, in their artistic lifetimes, for the simple reason that the extremity of the discipline they imposed upon themselves would prove, for the next generations of artists, too restrictive not to dismiss:

> My mother and father had the utmost contempt for painters who painted things out of their heads. Not that they wanted to paint what is sometimes called photographically; far from it. They wanted to "render the object"—an immensely subtle process involving the interplay of the painter's subjective view with the way the light actually fell upon the object. The conflict—rather, the marriage—of objectivity and subjectivity was what made art such a wildly exciting and magical thing to my parents that they cared about literally nothing else, except maybe me.[8]

The "maybe" is immensely moving, for it notes the way her parents' contempt for others who did not share their religion of art might even have been visited on her, along with their transfer into her of the feeling that others did not value the Hales as much as they deserved. She solved both problems, of course, by making them the subject of her own substantial art. But in the process, she forces herself to reflection on the cold side of her mother. It comes through, notably, in her mother's famous "colds," which caused the beautiful artist to take to her bed and absolutely withhold herself from availability, even at times (like the first weekend Nancy would have been able to leave Dr. Hinkle's sanatorium for a "home" visit) that few could find appropriate.

[8] Ibid. 20

Nancy's own solution, in these pages, is to love her mother in an analytic way, piece by piece (her last words to Lilian the night before she dies are "I love you to pieces"), and her method for doing this, as it was in feeling into her father's creative impasses and seeing how different they were from her own, is empathy. Empathy, the ability to see what the other feels, leads her again and again into remarkable resonance with the concerns of the vanishing breed her parents had become for most people interested in serious art in the early 1960s, when the bulk of these reflections were written. Her father, who had died in 1931, was "fond of declaring that modernists—meaning painters since Cézanne—were in effect saying, 'Let me look into the interior of my belly.'" [9] Thirty years later, Nancy was able to say on behalf of her mother, who wouldn't have been able to articulate what she felt so heartbreakingly clearly:

> That attitude in modern painting was what profoundly distressed her. It was not at all that modern pictures were abstractions. "Every good painting is basically an abstraction," my father used to say. Or that they were not representational. Her display was different from the layman's display. What depressed her was the loss of that rapturous meeting between the artist's private vision and the shimmering world of objects. To her it amounted to a loss of soul. [10]

The word "soul" is extraordinarily apt. Her mother's theory and practice of art was finally a religious activity, one Nancy Hale herself managed to carry forward in a psychological way. With this variety of religious experience in mind, the family consciousness that emerges is one we might want to call Jamesian (if the word may be extended to include the earnest pragmatism of William alongside the aesthetic sensibility of Henry James). The way Nancy Hale never leaves her own subjectivity out when

---

[9] Ibid. 27

[10] Ibid.

taking up the task of achieving an objective view of her parents gives her view of them enormous poignancy. By her book's end, she has solved that puzzle in a very pleasing way, locating each piece in relation to each other one (the actual pieces need to be read in turn to be appreciated, and I will not pre-empt that pleasure for a reader by summarizing them here) but what is not included in Nancy's answer, satisfying as it is, is the source of the patient love that has enabled her to persevere in connecting the individual pieces. For it is, I think, love, and not just a post-analytic effort at full self-healing, that has enabled her to put together the legacy she has received. Nancy Hale would probably have refused to conceive that love as not somehow stemming from her parents, since it is beautiful, and beauty is something she feels she found only through them. After all, they were artists, trained in appreciating beauty. In her final chapter, "An Arrangement in Parents," she tries to repay what she feels she owes them in this regard by deftly explaining their complicated marriage through a garden image—a rose tree and its standard—which becomes for her a "true lover's knot, for true lovers all to admire." [11] At the same time, however, the reader is entitled to feel that, by dint of having written this book, a lonely, sometimes forgotten child has finally found her way past being only her parents' daughter. Perhaps I project the psychological orphan in me that felt so immediately at home with the Hales so many years ago, but I find a companion in the consciousness that threads through this book, trying to sample her original home in a finally pleasing way. Like the sewing Nancy claims that she has no aptitude for, assigning that talent exclusively to her mother, the invisible thread of a generous intuition has all along seen the point in working out what her parents were really like so that she can finally be at home with them. Nancy Hale would not have elected to turn such an individual

---

[11] *The Life in the Studio* 209

journey into a formula, but she was nevertheless teasing out a home truth in *The Life in the Studio* as to how to make our lives that I believe can be worded as a pair of propositions. I find them to be linked, in the logical structure of this book, just as Nancy's parents were in life. I hope I may be forgiven for numbering (and naming) their relative views. I do so because I believe they constitute the legacy Nancy was able to receive and pass on to us in this remarkable book about what the artists she knew found important to do with their lives, thereby contributing to the art of living for all of us:

1 (Philip). Not a bad way to move our own lives forward is to take up the projects our forebears have left behind.

2 (Lilian). That's true, and it's fine to do so for as long as it takes us to find out what those were, for that's the surest way to discover what the people we have loved were really about.

Works Cited

Hale, Nancy. *A New England Girlhood*. Boston & Toronto: Little, Brown & Company, 1958.

——————. *The Life in the Studio*. Boston & Toronto: Little, Brown & Company, 1969.

"'In Eulogy of Emerson,' Dr. Edward Everett Hale's Address Before a Brooklyn Audience," *New York Times*, May 26, 1893.

JOHN BEEBE, M.D., is a Jungian analyst, editor of the *San Francisco Jung Library Journal*, co-editor of the *Journal of Analytical Psychology*, and an expert on psychological types. He is former President of the C.G. Jung Institute of San Francisco, where he is currently on the teaching faculty, as well as Assistant Clinical Professor of Psychiatry at the University of California Medical School, San Francisco.

Nancy Hale
(6 May 1908 – 24 September 1988)

Anne Hobson Freeman

⸺∞⸺

In the late 1970s Nancy Hale used to come to my writing class once every semester. She would sweep regally into the classroom—back ramrod straight under a smartly cut suit, angel hair billowing above her finely chiseled face. The students would be speechless with surprise, and Nancy with shyness, as I struggled lamely to introduce her.

Silence would then fall upon the room. Nancy, sitting next to me at the end of the long seminar table, would unfold her tortoise-shell half-glasses and set them just below the rise of that magnificent nose. Peering down its slope, she would then begin to read something she had written.

Her well-chosen words—so pure, precise, and yet endlessly surprising—intoned by that inimitable voice, with its hollow echoes and occasional broad *a*'s, would carry us back to the Boston of her childhood. And *up*, too, toward a standard of expression that every writer in that room longed, someday, to achieve. The standard was, quite simply, perfection.

By that time she had published eighteen books and scores of short stories, primarily in *The New Yorker* magazine. And she was now hard at work on a historical novel based on the life and letters of her great-uncle Charles Hale. The chasm of achievement that separated her from us seemed unbridgeable, until her words began to work their magic.

By the time she took those reading glasses off and folded them back into their case, the students knew and loved, and now, inexplicably, felt obliged to protect the vulnerable soul that had been so starkly revealed.

In the aftermath of revelation, Nancy was surprisingly relaxed. As she responded to questions on her favorite subject—the mystery of writing—her spontaneity, frankness, and total engagement suggested that she saw herself as just another writer talking to her equals.

The students loved her for it. They would go home and write into their journals words like "gutsy," "queenly," "dangerously honest," or "as beautiful inside, as she is on the outside." One, who later became a fiction editor at *Mademoiselle*, wrote, "I wish that Nancy Hale was my grandmother. Then I could talk to her like that anytime I wanted to."

A fact that always surfaced in those classroom discussions was that the fiction writer must be brave enough to probe for the very personal discovery, the inner secret that turns out to be the main reason the fiction writer writes and the fiction reader reads.

Nancy Hale made this observation more formally in *The Realities of Fiction* (1962) when she said: "Stories of mine that have made readers say, 'Why! That's just the way it is with me!' seem, to my surprise, to be about what I should have thought most private, most personal to myself. Just so I seem to do better by the world when I am acting for what is most inwardly myself."

That statement might be used now as a touchstone to determine which among the hundred short stories, forty-odd memoirs, and seven novels Nancy Hale published over half a century will be lasting contributions to the world of letters.

As long as she remained in contact with the well of feeling, deep below the surface, and let that feeling generate the form of her writing, she produced wonderful short stories, and memoirs that broke new ground for the prose elegy. But when she came at writing from the opposite direction, from the head and not the heart, she was much less successful. The intellectual constructs she felt obliged to impose on her novels and many of her stories—theses based on rigid and reductive assumptions about the northerner's versus the southerner's response, of the academic's versus the artist's—diminished the power of her talent.

Admittedly these contrasts fueled some brilliant satire. One of the funniest scenes in modern literature is the literary cocktail party in New York attended by the author from Virginia in *Dear Beast* (1959). Small wonder William Faulkner went out of his way to compliment "Miss Nancy" on that particular performance. Yet even here, in her satire, the touchstone can be applied to distinguish the shallow kind that masked her anger and antagonism from the all-embracing kind that sprang from pure delight in human foibles. Her most daring experiment in satire, *Heaven and Hardpan Farm* (1957), is set in a mental institution. Yet it works, because her portraits of the patients and their Jungian doctor are bathed in that redemptive delight.

In reality as well as fiction, Nancy Hale indulged in at least two kinds of laughter—a tinny social laugh which signaled lack of ease and a deep and lovely rumble that bubbled from her soul. When all is said and done, though, it was not in satire but in celebration that her talent found its fullest expression.

The books I find myself going back to reread now are the quiet and deliciously sensuous stories in *The Earliest Dreams* (1936), *Between the Dark and the Daylight* (1943), *The Empress's Ring* (1955), and *The Pattern of Perfection* (1960), the odes to childhood in *A New England Girlhood* (1958) and *Secrets* (1971), and the elegies to her parents and her aunt in *The Life in the Studio* (1969).

The writer of a tribute in the London *Times* the week after her death concluded that "Nancy Hale was a miniaturist whose imagination was at its best when playing on everyday problems and minor tragedies.... On the whole Miss Hale was not as successful on the largest canvas of the novel as she was in the short stories. The carefully polished prose, so effective at setting scenes... tended to drown in over luxuriance when asked to explore powerful conflicts and deep emotions."

Her best-known novel, *The Prodigal Women* (1942), is, however, a notable exception. Though the writing of that book consumed five years of her life and wrecked her health, it was a critical success as well as a best-seller. And it proved that her talent could be stretched to the wide canvas. As André Maurois pointed out in his preface to the French translation of the novel, like Tolstoy, she knew "how to develop a company of numerous destinies and to move them in an authentic social setting."

The author herself was slightly apprehensive about the reissue of *The Prodigal Women*. She had come a long way spiritually, as well as technically, from the thirty-five-year-old sophisticate who had wrestled with that rich, unwieldy book. In her maturity, she learned to use her gift—for bringing scenes and characters abundantly to life through color, shape, texture, smell, and sound—with greater discipline.

~

In 1980 a stroke changed Nancy's life dramatically. For fifty years writing had been her *raison d'être*. Now it was relegated to secondary status as she struggled to regain the use of the left side of her body. For the first time in her life, she developed a passionate interest in athletics. Physical therapy came first now, before even her writing, every morning. By the end of a year, she had managed to regain eighty-five percent of her physical powers, but she would walk with a slight limp and a cane for the rest of her life.

There were falls and other setbacks still to come. And breakthroughs, too. As she explained in an unpublished essay on her illness, "You don't speak of a stroke as anything you have totally conquered. It is work in progress."

Through the fall and winter of 1980-1981, despite the rigors of her physical therapy program, she doggedly pushed through to completion the second draft of "Charlieshope." "A novel-in-history" is the term she coined for this ambitious work. It was a blending of the letters of her uncle Charles Hale, former editor of the *Boston Daily Advertiser* and U.S. consul general to Egypt, with her own memories of the tales her father used to tell her about the slightly Bohemian household he and his brothers and sisters—known in Boston as "the Dirty Delightfuls"—had grown up in.

The book gave her a chance to celebrate the childhood of her father, the painter Philip Hale, and to portray her grandfather, the leonine and beloved Unitarian minister who wrote *The Man Without a Country* (1863). But it also sapped her energy at a critical point in her recovery and depressed her spirit as she relived (through the writing of the last few chapters) her great-uncle's final debilitating illness. She began to believe that his illness might have been a punishment for sins earlier in his life.

The oppressive morality of the Victorians, Nancy Hale would be the first to admit, has no place in modern fiction. Yet she identified, too closely probably, with the characters she wrote about, and at that point in her own life she lacked the energy to resist the negative pull of that particular book. In the throes of those last chapters, she began to question the value of writing as a way of life and to wonder if it might not be a "sinful occupation."

In May 1981 her editor sent back the second draft of "Charlieshope" with suggestions for a final editing, and Nancy decided that she did not have the strength, physically or psychologically, to run the manuscript through her typewriter again. She returned the advance and thereby bought her freedom from the book and ultimately from the despair that was associated with it.

Her decision was a wise one, for within a month she was hospitalized again with an aftermath of the stroke, an illness whose acronym was SIEADH and whose symptoms brought her to the brink of death. Every modicum of energy she still retained, she needed to pull herself back from that, the severest of her setbacks.

Yet she had meant what she said in a newspaper interview: "I'd rather choke, than stop writing." For her, writing was as essential as breathing; it was the means by which she had learned to cope with the harshest realities of life. As she wrote once in her notebook: "Creative writing is for the sublimation of the unendurable." And so, despite the stroke and SIEADH, through the 1980s she continued to produce short stories and memoirs in a thin but steady stream.

In "Tastes," which appeared in the Autumn 1982 *Virginia Quarterly Review*, she explored the positive reaction to debilitating illness which her widowed Aunt Nancy exemplified. The memoir opens with the statement: "Increasingly—perhaps because there are so few of her sort around any more—I think of my Aunt Nancy. My first, golden picture of her is before she was married: golden, curly hair ablaze, singing in her high and happy voice, 'Yip I Yaddy I Yoodly Yay.' It was about 1913; I would have been five."

It closes with a visit to the "infinitely cheerless" nursing home where her aunt lay confined to her bed with osteoporosis, looking over old family photographs and postcards.

> To her apparently they were perennially fresh and interesting.... After we had spoken about how we missed my mother, we turned to other memories and laughed a lot. At one point, suddenly incredibly, Aunt Nancy exclaimed, "When I first wake up in the morning I'm so happy I could *squeal.*"
> Yip I Yaddy I Yoodly Yay.

Coming when it did, right after her own illnesses, the piece represented a spiritual breakthrough for its author. She had managed to reverse the negative direction of her thoughts about old age and illness and writing as a way of life. And she did it by connecting, once again, with her secret source.

Afterwards, when she recalled her despair after the writing of "Charlieshope," she said, "When I'm writing well, I don't feel sinful. I feel blessed."

By 1984 she had found out that her grandsons were dyslexic and was trying to find out how she could help them—and children like them—learn to love reading the way she always had. In the process, she discovered that there is a dearth of emotionally satisfying stories with the short sentences and strong narrative thread such children need to get them started. And so she set about to write some for them.

After studying the material the Center for Dyslexia in Charlottesville sent to her, she wrote to one of their tutors, Sheelah Scott: "The description of unhappy, losing children in the teaching book touched me deeply. There is something about a child who feels he is failing which is absolutely unbearable. I'm so glad you can help them and hope I can too."

In the end she produced eighteen children's stories, drawing details from her own childhood and that of her children and her grandchildren. Frequently she used the old stone house and studio, Howlets (her summer home in Folly Cove, Massachusetts), as the setting. Her aim was always to encourage the child who was having difficulty adjusting, but also to make the story attractive. As she saw it, "the trouble for many of these children [was] that reading just hasn't been made seductive to them.... Children want to fly in fancy. Over the most trivial matters."

"Birds in the House" was the first of the three booklets published in Charlottesville by the Learning Center in 1985. In it a ten-year-old girl identifies with two birds that are temporarily trapped in her house. Eventually she finds relief from her own disappointment by climbing to her favorite place in an apple tree and writing in her journal. The story ends triumphantly with the girl's discovery that no matter what happened to her "she could always do that—look at the things around her and write them down."

In the second story, "Wags," written for an even younger reader, a cocker spaniel very narrowly escapes drowning at Folly Cove. The author, trying to confine herself to one-syllable words, said that she experienced a thrill of victory when she thought of describing the glacial boulders in the cove as "Ice Age rocks."

Nancy Hale's last published work was "Miss Dugan," an homage to her high-school English teacher, in the anthology *An Apple for My Teacher* (1987, Algonquin Books). She claimed that Miss Dugan had "saved her life" her first year at the Winsor School in Boston by taking an interest in her poetry when she was "drowning in seas of inferiority, shyness (that unfortunately did not look like shyness but rather antagonism), and despair." At the end, the author reciprocates many years later, when the two of them are swimming in a stone quarry up the road from Folly Cove. To Nancy Hale the image of water—whether it was in the sea, a quarry, or even a swimming pool—represented the unconscious, the chaos that threatens all of us, but particularly artists who have to plunge into it every day to do their work. In her notebook she had written: "There isn't any question (in my feeling) but that the world is more attractive than to create, i.e. I'd rather live than write. But without creation one would get lost in the unconscious—the sea."

Neither Nancy nor Miss Dugan was a very confident swimmer. On this occasion they had strayed perilously close to the deepest water, where the shelf of granite, almost six feet underneath them, was abruptly sheered. Miss Dugan had been happily floating on her back when:

> Suddenly I observed something queer. Miss Dugan was making so little effort to swim that she was, actually, sinking. Her legs were drifting downwards so that they were almost vertical. Her head, tipped back, was beginning to sink. Her chin was under water.
>
> I realized abruptly that unless I did something, quick, Miss Dugan was going to drown…. I've got to save her, I thought. By letting my feet down I found I could just touch bottom on tiptoe. Reaching out, I took hold of Miss Dugan's inertly drifting hand. "Hold on to me" I commanded her. I was not sure she could hear. "Just don't grab me! If you hold my hand I can pull you in."
>
> Miss Dugan held on. For a moment it seemed infinitely perilous—I was so near the brink of the really deep water, where I would not be able to help her. Then I found surer footing, and began pulling Miss Dugan, whose body moved lightly in the water, on to the shore. She told me afterward she had only been repeating Blake.

The method Nancy Hale used to rescue her old teacher was a very light one, all that she could manage, imperiled as she was by her own lack of strength in the deep water. It resembles very closely the method that she used in her best writing and attempted to describe when an English bibliographer asked her for a comment on her work: "I am averse to making statements on my work," she wrote, "because I have found by experience that fiction is so protean that today's aim can be tomorrow's anathema. But I may make the comment that in general I have striven to conceal the purpose underlying my work with 'the light touch' since nothing seems to me so self-defeating as overt earnestness. Yet I can assure readers of my work that its purpose is earnest, indeed painful."

In April 1988 she suffered a second, minor stroke and spent most of her last summer at Folly Cove overcoming the indignities of it. She had virtually won that battle, too, by the time she and her husband, Fredson Bowers, returned to Charlottesville at the end of August.

As I sat beside her on the airplane coming home—while her husband drove the car, packed to the roof with their belongings and their works-in-progress—I suddenly turned to her and said, "You really are a good sport, Nancy."

"I have no alternative," she said quietly.

The week before she died, she urged her physical therapist to give her harder exercises, started on a series of Italian lessons, and dictated the first draft of a story. She was fully alive and fighting back the only way Nancy Hale knew how to fight, which was with all her might, when the final stroke carried her away on the twenty-fourth of September 1988.

As I was leafing through an old *Who's Who* the next morning for biographical facts to include in the obituary notice, I came upon a statement which Nancy, herself, had appended to her entry: "After a long and reflective life, my impression is that the life itself is seeking a goal & whether in art or in reality, the sign of creation having been present ... is a sensation of pure joy."

Those last two words, "pure joy," cut right to the core, as Nancy's words could do, beyond the sense of loss and grief, to suggest the final response of her friends and many of her readers to her presence on this earth for eighty years.

1988

ANNE HOBSON FREEMAN is the author of *The Style of a Law Firm: Eight Gentlemen from Virginia* and *A Hand Well Played: The Life of Jim Wheat, Jr.*, and editor of Mary Lee Settle's *Learning to Fly: A Writer's Memoir*. Her own stories have been published in numerous journals and anthologies including *Virginia Quarterly Review* and *The Best American Short Stories*.

About the Series:

Volumes in the Unsung Masters Series are published once a year by Pleiades Press (as long as funding allows) and feature work by, and essays on, unjustly neglected or out-of-print writers. Each volume in the series is distributed free to *Pleiades* magazine subscribers with the summer (June) issue. Unsung Masters Series book are also available through Small Press Distribution.

Volume 1, *Dunstan Thompson: On the Life & Work of a Lost American Master*, edited by D. A. Powell & Kevin Prufer, 2010

Volume 2, *Tamura Ryuichi: On the Life & Work of a 20th Century Master*, edited by Takako Lento & Wayne Miller, 2011

Volume 3, *Nancy Hale: On the Life & Work of a Lost American Master*, edited by Dan Chaon, Norah Hardin Lind, & Phong Nguyen, 2012

Volume 4, on Russell Atkins, edited by Michael Dumanis & Kevin Prufer, will be published in 2013

Volume 5, on Francis Jammes, edited by Kathryn Nuernberger, will be published in 2014

Series editors: Wayne Miller, Phong Nguyen, & Kevin Prufer